Becoming a Therapist

Personal development is fundamental to professional development and therapeutic practice. Until now, the unstructured personal or reflective journal has by default become the sole vehicle for recording reflection through training.

Becoming a Therapist is a unique practical manual, facilitating the movement and growth of the reader while raising awareness of resistance to change. With challenging questions and exercises, it forces the reader to consider his or her own personal value systems, strengths and limitations as they relate to the practice of therapy, tackling vital issues such as:

- Family
- Culture
- Gender
- Ethics

Indispensable to counsellors, counselling psychologists and psychotherapists in training, *Becoming a Therapist* is a thought-provoking companion to personal and professional development.

Malcolm Cross is a Senior Lecturer in Counselling Psychology and Director of Counselling Psychology Programmes at City University, London. **Linda Papadopoulos** is a Senior Lecturer and Course Director in Counselling Psychology at London Guildhall University, London.

Becoming a Therapist

A MANUAL FOR PERSONAL AND PROFESSIONAL DEVELOPMENT

Malcolm C. Cross
and
Linda Papadopoulos

BRUNNER-ROUTLEDGE
ALERE FLAMMAM
Taylor & Francis Group

First published 2001
by Brunner-Routledge
27 Church Road, Hove, East Sussex BN3 2FA

Simultaneously published in the USA and Canada
by Taylor and Francis Inc.
29 West 35th Street, New York, NY 10001

Brunner-Routledge is an imprint of the Taylor and Francis Group

Typeset in Goudy by Keystroke, Jacaranda Lodge, Wolverhampton
Printed and bound in Great Britain by Biddles Ltd, Guildford and
King's Lynn
Cover design by Richard Massing

British Library Cataloguing in Publication Data
A catalogue record for this book is available from the British Library

Library of Congress Cataloging-in-Publication Data
Cross, Malcolm C., 1966–
  Becoming a therapist : a manual for personal and professional development/
  Malcolm C. Cross, Linda Papadopoulos.
    p. cm.
  Includes bibliographical references and index.
  ISBN 0–415–22115–3 (pbk.)
  1. Counselors—Training of. 2. Counseling—Study and teaching. I. Papadopoulos,
Linda, II. Title.

BF637.C6 C743 2001
158′.3′023—dc21   2001025648

ISBN 0–415–22115–3 (pbk)

Contents

Figures

Introduction

INTRODUCTION

Personal development is a process of recursive and ongoing integration. It requires openness to experience, a commitment to experiment, an engagement with the world and a critical reflection on experience. It is about knowing yourself and understanding how your experience shapes your subsequent encounters with the world. Personal development is of critical importance for counsellors and therapists as they participate in the process of helping.[1]

Self-knowledge or personal insight enables you to avoid personal blind spots and develop trust in your observations and confidence in your practice. This manual aims to facilitate the process of personal and professional development through enhancing self-knowledge and fostering insight. You will be encouraged to reflect on how your experiences, values and beliefs may impact on your practice. Self-knowledge is a resource in the practice of helping. The manual provides a range of opportunities for you to explore landmark events in your past and determine what implications these have for who you are and how you practise as a therapist.

Landmark experiences are those which, on reflection, you name as shaping, moulding or influencing who you are. They are events or happenings that have a lasting impact on us. These events may challenge our existing view of the world or provide us with powerful confirmatory evidence, assuring us that our theories hold and our beliefs are valid. We remember these events because they either confirm our view of ourselves as we are today or they stand at odds with who we seek to become. Landmark events may arise in the context of our families, communities and intimate relationships. These contexts are explored in Chapters 2, 3 and 4 dealing with the topics of family, culture and gender respectively. These experiences are often invaluable observational platforms in the struggle to gain insight into our own personal perspectives.

---

1 Despite their differing education and training background, the capacity of therapists to reflect insightfully and critically on self, in the helping relationship, is of fundamental importance to the helping process. For this reason we have chosen to use the terms *counsellor* and *therapist* interchangeably throughout this manual.

A useful model for conceptualising the process of personal development is Kelly's (1991) experience cycle (Figure 1.1). Change in general and personal and professional development in particular can be understood in terms of the five phases outlined in Kelly's model.

At the *anticipation* stage the person looks towards what is to come. Clearly some anticipatory stances are more helpful than others in terms of their utility in processes of change, growth and learning. A dismissive, disengaged or uninterested posture closes one to experience, as does certainty. In an effort to maximise the potential of the manual, you are encouraged to be open and engage with the material.

Commitment in the cycle of experience implies self-involvement. It requires you to view the material you encounter as an opportunity, with potential to shape who you are and how you see yourself. As you work through the manual, this phase of the cycle of growth may take the form of questions you ask yourself such as: *What can I learn about myself and my potential to practise from this exercise?*

The *encounter* stage of Kelly's experience cycle suggests engagement and participation in the material at an intellectual and emotional level. As you work through the manual, this stage of the process of personal and professional development will be manifest in questions such as: *How do I genuinely feel about this at the deepest level? Did I expect this outcome and what does this mean for me today, tomorrow, as a trainee therapist and ultimately an independent practitioner?*

Confirmation and *disconfirmation* refer to your evaluation of the stages of anticipation, commitment and encounter in terms of the outcome of your experiment. Did things turn out as you predicted? Have the exercises brought into your awareness challenges, opportunities and contradictions that previously escaped your attention? In view of these insights, what theories about yourself or others need to be revised or fine tuned? Or has this experiment strengthened your resolve or certainty regarding your previously held perspective on particular events?

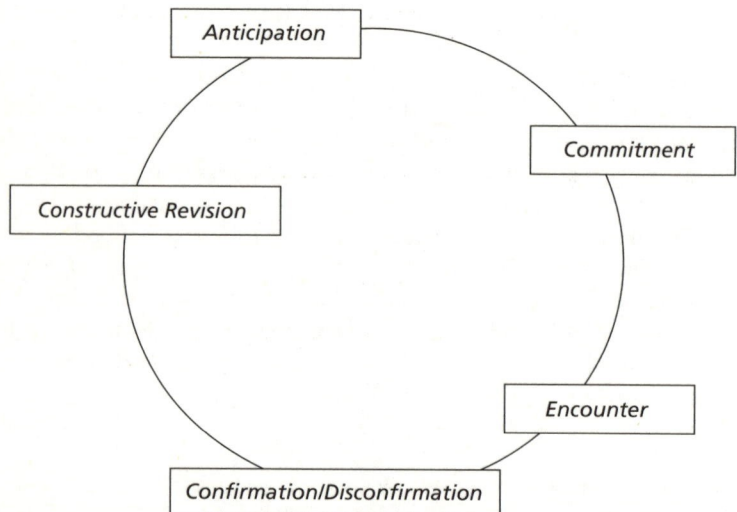

Figure 1.1 Kelly's experience cycle *Source: Kelly (1991)*

The answers to questions such as these are likely to facilitate the resolution of the final stage of the experience cycle, that of *constructive revision*.

Personal and professional development is not a one-off event or activity. As the experience cycle implies, personal and professional development is continuous and ongoing. Within this model each revolution is both informed by the encounters of the past and in turn shapes our encounters with the future. The manual and its contents are just one opportunity to develop a deeper understanding of yourself in this lifelong process.

If we are successful in knowing the impact of events on us, we can begin to appreciate the unique nature of our own perspective on experience. We interrupt the process of causality. Causality in this context is the process of uncritically imbuing particular objects or events with meaning. For example, should we encounter a particular event and experience positive, negative or indifferent feelings, the event is labelled good, bad or indifferent. The feeling becomes a quality of the event rather than the property of the observer. Thinking through the origins of our feelings, our first or pivotal encounters with a significant event can free us from having to experience events in only one way. This process of separating event from meaning enables us to step back from our experience and entertain alternative possibilities. The idea that the same event can be experienced differently over time and differently by others has important implications for therapy. This is a recurring theme within the manual and one to which we will often return.

It is possible to tell stories rather than live them. This is sometimes referred to as living inauthentically. The manual will provide you with the opportunity to fully engage with and be challenged by the material. Equally however, the manual could be completed as a passionless exercise, a checklist or tedious inventory. These options are open to you; however, nowhere could the cliché 'You will only stand to gain what you invest' be more relevant. Such risks in investment place special responsibilities on the entrepreneur. Look after your assets; that is, keep yourself and your manual safe. Some exercises may encourage you to recall painful and provocative experiences. This being the case you should determine a priori strategies to best care for yourself. From whom would you seek support and debriefing if you felt it necessary? Where are you going to keep your manual? The content of the manual should be yours alone – unless you choose to share it.

PERSONAL DEVELOPMENT AND PROFESSIONAL PRACTICE

The text and exercises in this manual seek to minimise the chances of your unintentionally making the client victim of your own needs for validation. You will be encouraged to develop the skill of processing on multiple levels, as one does when one seeks to monitor and be in the therapeutic encounter at the same time. You will gain practice in examining events from a range of perspectives and develop an understanding of why you view events in the way you do, and why change may be challenging and sometimes elusive. These insights are of clear relevance to the work of a therapist.

Through engagement with this manual, it is hoped that you will move closer to a stance of openness and confidence. Your curiosity will be stimulated and your understanding of your personal motivation to help will be enhanced. The importance of such personal achievements for the ethical practice of therapy is plain and will be explored in more detail in Chapter 5 focusing on morals, values and ethics. In Chapter 6 you will be afforded the opportunity to appraise your own personal strengths and weaknesses and evaluate their potential impact on your capacity to help.

Each chapter of the manual focuses on a topic of relevance to the practice of therapy. Contained within each topic is background information and theory interspersed with experiential exercises designed to make the material personally meaningful. You should work your way though the exercises at your own pace. You are encouraged to use the manual as a guide and reflective journal. Make memos and notes to yourself often. The significance of these entries may only occur to you later as patterns emerge over time and across seemingly different contexts.

Should you have difficulties engaging with the manual, such as feeling that some topic areas are too painful or provocative, ask yourself how best to move this forward? It may be that personal therapy would be the appropriate venue for you to work through particularly difficult areas of your life. The contact details of major bodies for the registration of counsellors, psychologists and psychotherapists are provided as an appendix at the end of this book. Acknowledgement of an area of personal difficulty is a victory. It is the first step towards acceptance, accommodation and resolution. Notice too if you feel bored or tired. Remember that the exercises are merely containers or frameworks within which to place your own material. If you are tired, bored or find your attention wandering, ask yourself: *What am I avoiding here? Do I really think that I am that dull? Do I have the personal space to engage with this material right now?* Be aware of when you are overly intellectualising the exercises. As you work your way through the material stop from time to time to review what you have written and ask yourself: *Do I really feel that?* Change and resistance to change are explored in Chapter 7.

It is equally important to have·fun. There is a common misconception that all things of value are hard won. Personal development through self-knowledge and insight can be a source of excitement and amusement. Take frequent breaks and give yourself time to reflect on and digest the work you have done. Nurture and support yourself, as you will encourage your clients to do in your work with them.

2

Family

What does my family have to do with my practice as a therapist?

No experience occurs in a vacuum; we are all influenced by and influence our surroundings. Life events such as birth, illness, marriage and death alter not only *inter*personal relationships but also *intra*personal climates, affecting our perceptions of who we are and how we relate to those around us (Papadopoulos and Bor, 1995). One's family has the capacity to aid or hinder growth, to nurture or to stunt personal development and, perhaps most importantly, to provide a first glimpse into how we see ourselves as part of a larger social unit.

Our self-concept, self-esteem and even our prejudices may initially develop through the context of our family. There is a need therefore in our quest for personal development to go back and examine those events that have influenced our beliefs and personalities.

As individuals, examining the impact of family on our development will allow us to analyse family narratives upon which our daily experiences are based. As therapists it will allow us to see how our convictions of self, 'normality' and ethics affect and are affected by our interactions with clients.

This chapter will examine how familial beliefs, rituals and experiences can affect one's personal development. The importance of family 'narratives' will be underscored and the utility of a family map or genogram discussed. As you work through the chapter, make a conscious effort to look at how you feel when completing the different exercises. You may want to make notes on how your views on different issues change or are challenged by completing the different exercises. Finally, try to be as accurate and honest as possible when completing the exercises; if you are uncertain about the sequence of particular events, enlist help from someone in the family who does.

DEFINING FAMILY

The first step in our journey towards personal development is to define what we mean by the term *family*. At first sight this may seem a simple task; however, our definition here does not assume a biological relationship, but rather includes close social unions between two or more people. The essence of the 'family system' was captured in Buckley's (1967) definition, which identifies a system as being made up of sets of different parts with two common features. First, the parts are connected and dependent on each other, and second, each part of the system is related to the other over time. Drawing from this definition, it becomes apparent that the wholeness, which the family possesses, means that it is not merely the sum of parts taken separately but rather includes the interaction of those parts. Thus one cannot understand a given part without taking into account its interaction with other parts (Papadopoulos and Bor, 1995).

Having read the above definition, think of how you define family in your own words and complete sections A and B below.

EXERCISE

(A) Define 'family' in your own words:

....

....

....

....

....

....

....

(B) Who does your family system comprise of?

....

....

....

....

....

....

....

....

Look at your answers for A and B and think about where your definition has derived from. Perhaps your definition has a cultural significance, or perhaps it is related to the beliefs of a particular family member. Think about how easy or difficult it was to come up with your answers, and whether you are satisfied with the definitions given above. It may be the case that you have identified a non-biological acquaintance in your family list, or that you have had to redefine your notion of family to account for who you have included. Make a point of returning to the list while you go through the rest of the exercises and see if you feel the need to add or subtract names as you progress.

Your answers thus far will have given you some insight into who some of the most significant people in your family are. Now look at the list below, and for each of the descriptive words on the left think of the family member who comes to mind and put their name in the blank on the right. If none of the descriptive words applies to individual family members, create your own list and identify a family member for each word.

(C)

Anchor ....

Balance ....

Calm ....

Inspiration ....

Fire ....

Laughter ....

Difficult ....

Angry ....

Different ....

Like me ....

Unlike me ....

————— ....

————— ....

————— ....

————— ....

————— ....

Look at your list, and remind yourself why you chose the descriptives for each person in your family. Was your choice based on one salient event or on a series of experiences that you remember?

....

....

....

....

....

....

....

....

Are there cases where a family member has changed over time?

....

....

....

....

Do you think that the descriptive list you are using today is different to the one you would have chosen in the past? If this is the case, think of why and when the change occurred and make notes below.

....

....

....

....

....

(D) Think of five words that best describe you and list them below.

....

....

....

....

....

Are you the first person to describe yourself using these words, or has someone else described you with these words in the past?

Yes ☐
No ☐

If so, who described you using this word and in what situation did this take place?

....

....

....

....

....

For each person you have identified in your family list, give two words that they would use to describe you.

FAMILY MEMBER	DESCRIPTIVE WORDS	
_____	....	....
_____	....	....
_____	....	....
_____	....	....
_____	....	....

Do you agree with the descriptives given above? Which do you agree with most and which do you agree with least?

....

....

....

....

....

For each person on the above list, ask them to give two words that best describe you, and compare these with the descriptives that you have chosen. Take notes of similarities and differences, and give possible explanations as to why these exist. In cases where you are unclear about the descriptive given by a family member, ask them to explain why they chose to use that particular word.

PUTTING THE PAST IN PLACE

As a trainee therapist, one of the issues that will often arise with clients and indeed in your own personal development is the need to examine the way significant past life events have impacted upon behaviour and personality. Many of the established psychotherapy models have at their core a historical approach to personality development and psychopathology (Corsini, 1981). By discovering and examining the past, we are able to lay foundations for the future and to address problems, conflicts or negative patterns that may have otherwise gone unnoticed or unchallenged. In many cases, simply acknowledging or naming a particular life event can be enough to allow us to 'make sense of' the event and to change the way it is impacting upon our lives. Research suggests that many of our established belief patterns about ourselves and society as a whole are related to our experiences and perceptions of past life events (Beck, 1976). As such, these events can significantly affect self-esteem and self-concept and in some cases impose false limits on our beliefs of what we can or cannot achieve. Furthermore, an unresolved family conflict or emotional family issue can taint the way we perceive similar problems. This may be particularly relevant when we are faced with a client whose problem resonates with an unresolved issue or life event that we ourselves have experienced.

The purpose of the following exercise is to allow you to examine which events have significantly affected your personal development, and to examine their potential for affecting your professional development.

(E1) Think back and identify three events that occurred – one during childhood, one during adolescence and one in adulthood – that you feel have significantly impacted upon your personal development:

....

....

....

....

....

....

....

(E2) For each of the events you have listed above, discuss why you thought it was important, and what effect, if any, you think this event had on other members of your family.

....

....

....

....

....

....

....

....

(F) Speak to the individuals involved in each of the events of 'E' above and compare their perception of events to yours.

How are these similar or different?

....

....

....

....

....

....

....

....

Whose stories are the closest to yours and whose are furthest away?

....

....

....

....

....

The above exercise is intended to highlight the way in which family members' interpretations develop and also to underscore the importance of 'subjective perceptions' whereby the same event can be interpreted in a variety of different ways depending on one's beliefs, expectations and past experiences. Theorists who work with the cognitive model of therapy posit that it is not situations in and of themselves that are stressful but rather our perceptions of each particular experience. In a similar vein, family perceptions of right and wrong or good and bad may not necessarily conform to views of an individual family member or indeed society as a whole. It is for this reason that examining perceptions of family and self are vital in our process of growth and professional development.

The following exercise is designed to highlight the importance of subjective interpretation within families.

(G) Ask each of the people described in 'E' to describe you and see how closely their descriptions relate to yours.

....

....

....

....

....

(H) Find a childhood photo of yourself; tell the story behind it. Who took the picture? Where were you living at the time? What happened prior to and after taking the picture?

....

....

....

....

....

The exercises set so far should have allowed you to understand that there is a great variation of accounts and beliefs in families. It is important to conceptualise that aspects of family life are viewed differently according to the positions of different members of the family.

GENOGRAMS

Genograms, or family trees, are an important clinical tool for many counsellors, therapists and other healthcare professionals and can be used for assessment, gathering information on family relationships and exploring themes in counselling practice. The information is displayed graphically and provides a quick reference to the often complex patterns of relationships that exist within families. The information contained in a genogram may include medical, behavioural, genetic, cultural and social aspects of the family system. Details of family history are taken and presented in a standard format using symbols (see p. 23). Names, ages, occupations and relationships are also entered. The geographic location of each of these people, siblings and other important family members are then recorded. Three or more generations of family members are included: their names, genders, dates of birth, marriage, divorce and death are all noted. Miscarriages, abortions, stillbirths, adoptions, separations, remarriages, infertility, disabilities, causes of death, significant legal problems, incest and education may also be included (Tomson, 1985).

Cultural and ethnic origins as well as religious affiliation may vary within the family and these need to be clarified, as they may be significant in developing both therapeutic questioning and an understanding of the family. The relationships between individuals included in the genogram are symbolically denoted by vertical and horizontal axes, lines of affinity and supplementary information. This information can also provide a rich source of hypotheses with regard to how a clinical problem may be linked to family history and relationships, and how a problem may evolve through time.

Genograms help to reveal patterns and events that may have recurring significance within a family system. McGoldrick and Gerson (1985) explain that the act of constructing a family diagram with a client or family that maps relationships and functioning patterns acts in a similar way as language does to potentiate and organise thought processes. To this end, genograms may be conceptualised both as a therapeutic intervention and a part of the process of counselling. They help counsellors conceptualise their clients' problems systematically, taking into account the way in which life events and relationships may be connected to family structure, beliefs and psychological problems as well as health and illness. Literature on the use and value of genograms in counselling has highlighted the efficacy of this tool from a number of perspectives. By obtaining an 'image' of the current family context, the counsellor can assess the family's strengths and weaknesses and can also examine relationship patterns between family members, addressing each member's connection or contribution to the so-called presenting problem. Further, the person labelled as having the problem can be viewed in the context of multiple systems such as their family, community, and broader sociocultural contexts (McGoldrick and Gerson, 1985), thereby introducing different frames through which to view problems.

Clarifying patterns of relationships within the family is one of the principal strengths of the genogram when used in a counselling context. As information is being collected to construct a genogram, the counsellor is given the opportunity to devise and revise hypotheses about relationships and problems. These hypotheses can then be put to family members who in turn are encouraged to offer their own perception of the so-called problem. Clarifying relationship patterns can also serve as an educational function for family members, since it may enable them to examine the way in which behaviour is connected to beliefs and feelings. An understanding of the connection between symptomatic behaviour and relationships within a family can empower family members to work towards their resolution. Indeed, once the family patterns which underlie problematic behaviour are identified, it is possible that the behaviour will change without the need for further psychotherapeutic intervention.

The genogram interview

Gathering information for the genogram usually occurs in the context of a family interview. Unless family members come in specifically to tell their family history for research purposes, you cannot simply gather genogram information and ignore the family's agenda for the interview. Such single-mindedness will not only hinder you in getting pertinent information, but also alienate the family from treatment. Gathering family information and constructing the genogram should form part of the more general task of helping the family.

The Rashomon effect

Genogram information may be obtained by interviewing one family member or several. Clearly, getting information from several family members increases reliability and provides the opportunity to compare perspectives and observe interactions directly. Often, when we interview several family members, we get what we call 'the Rashomon effect', based on a famous Japanese film where one event is shown from the point of view of a number of different characters. Similarly, we find in genogram interviews that family members tell different stories about the same events.

EXERCISE

What advantages and disadvantages does the Rashomon effect bring to the counselling process?

....

....

....

....

....

Of course, seeing several family members is not always feasible, and the interview described here can also be used with one person. The time required to complete a genogram assessment can vary greatly. While the basic information can usually be collected in less than half an hour, a comprehensive family assessment interview involving several family members may take from sixty to ninety minutes. Some clinicians prefer to spread the interviewing over a number of sessions.

The family information net

The actual process of gathering family information can be thought of as casting a metaphorical information net in ever wider circles in order to capture relevant information about the family and its broader context. The net spreads in a number of different directions:

- From the presenting problem to the larger context of the problem.
- From the immediate household to the extended family and broader social systems.
- From the present family situation to a historical chronology of family events.
- From easy, non-threatening queries to difficult, anxiety-provoking questions.
- From obvious facts to judgements about functioning and relationships to hypothesised family patterns.

The presenting problem and the immediate household

Family members usually present with specific problems, which should be the clinician's starting point. At the outset, we tell families that we need some basic information about them to fully understand the problem. Such information usually grows naturally out of exploring the presenting problem and its impact on the immediate household. It makes sense to most people for the clinician to ask about the immediate family and the context in which the problem occurs.

- Who lives in the household?
- How is each person related?
- Where do other family members live?

The clinician asks the name, age and sex of each person in the household in order to sketch the immediate family structure. Other revealing information can be elicited through enquiring about the problem:

- Which family members know about the problem?
- How does each view it and how has each member responded?
- Has anyone in the family ever had similar problems?
- What solutions were attempted by whom in those situations?

This is also a good time to enquire about previous efforts to seek help for the problem, including treatment, therapists, hospitalisations and the current referral source.

The current situation

Next, the clinician spreads the information net into the current family situation. This line of questioning usually follows naturally from questions about the problem and who is involved:

- What has been happening recently in your family?
- Have there been any recent changes in the family (people coming or leaving, illnesses, job problems, etc.)?

It is important to enquire about recent life-cycle transitions as well as anticipated changes in the family situation (especially exits and entries of family members – births, marriages, divorces, deaths, the departure of family members, etc.).

The clinician should look for an opportunity to explore the wider family context by asking about the extended family of all the adults involved. At a point in the discussion when the family seems at ease, the interviewer might say something like: 'I would now like to ask you something about your background to help make sense of your present problem.'

When family members react negatively to questions about the extended family or complain that such matters are irrelevant, it makes sense to redirect the focus back to the immediate situation until the connections between the present situation and other family relationships or experiences can be established. Gentle persistence over time will usually result in obtaining the information.

EXERCISE

List the ways that family members may react negatively to questions about the extended family.

....

....

....

....

....

What reasons might there be for family members to take umbrage at these lines of enquiry?

....

....

....

....

....

As a clinician, what do you think would be the best ways to respond to this negativity?

....

....

....

....

....

The clinician should enquire about each side of the family separately, beginning, for example with the mother's side:

- Let us begin with your mother's family. Your mother was which one of how many children?
- When was she born?
- Is she alive?
- [If not] when did she die?
- [If alive] where is she now? What does she do?
- Is she retired? When did this happen?

And so on. In like fashion, the same series of questions is asked about the father. The goal is to obtain information on three or four generations, including grandparents, parents, aunts, uncles, siblings, spouses and children of the person who is the focus of the genogram.

The social context

Enquiries should be made regarding friends, clergy, caretakers, teachers, doctors, etc. who are important to the functioning of the family, and this information should also be included in the genogram. In exploring outside support for the family, the clinician might ask the following:

- What roles have outside people played in your family?
- Have you received help from the community?
- Who, outside the family, has been important in your life?
- Has anyone else ever lived with your family? When? Where are they now?

What differences might you expect between clients' responses to family enquiries and their responses to social enquiries?

....

....

....

....

....

....

....

What reasons might there be for these differences and how might recognising these differences be useful to the therapeutic process?

....

....

....

....

....

....

....

....

Tracking family relationships and roles

While mapping on the genogram the nuclear and extended family and gathering facts on different family members, the clinician should also begin to make enquiries and judgements about the different types of relationships family members have and the functioning and roles of each person in the family. This involves going beyond

the bare facts to clinical judgement and acumen. Enquiries about family relationships, functioning and roles can touch quite sensitive nerves in the family
and should be made with care. Questions on relationships might include:

- Are there any family members who do not speak to each other or who have ever
  had a period of not speaking? Are there any who were/are in serious conflict?
- Are there any family members who are extremely close? Who helps out when
  help is needed? In whom do family members confide?
- All couples have some sort of marital difficulties. What sorts of problems and
  conflicts have you encountered? What about your parents' and siblings'
  marriages?
- How do you each get along with each child? Have any family members
  experienced particular problems dealing with their children?

EXERCISE |

Write down some more examples of questions on relationships that would
allow you to get as many perspectives on family relationships as possible.

....

....

....

....

....

....

....

....

....

....

....

How would you expect these enquiries to benefit the therapeutic process?

....

....

....

....

....

....

....

....

....

The goal is to uncover differences as well as agreements about family relationships and to use different perceptions of the family to enrich the genogram picture for both the therapist and the family.

Sometimes it is useful to ask how members of the present family would be characterised by other family members; for example, 'How do you think your older brother would describe your relationship with your wife?' or 'How would your father have described you when you were 13, the age your son is now?' Again, gathering as many perspectives as possible enriches the family's view of itself, and introducing differences provides channels for new information.

Difficult questions about individual functioning

Many family members may function well in some areas but not in others, or they may strive to mask their dysfunction. Often, it takes careful questioning to reveal the true level of functioning. Questions about individual functioning may be difficult or painful for family members to answer, and must be approached with sensitivity and tact. The family members should be warned that the questions may be difficult, and perhaps told to let the clinician know if an area is being touched that they would prefer not to discuss. The clinician will need to judge the degree of persistence to apply if family members resist such questions.

In the process of gathering information, the clinician should be aware of the types of patterns that may appear and probe for further information when such patterns are suggested by the data.

One of the most difficult aspects of genogram assessment remains the problem of setting priorities for inclusion of family information on a genogram. Clinicians cannot follow every lead that the genogram interview may suggest. Awareness of basic genogram patterns can help the clinician set such priorities. As a rule of thumb, the data are scanned for the following:

- Repetitive symptoms, relationships or functioning seen across the family and over the generations. Repeated triangles, coalitions, cut-offs, patterns of conflict, over- and under-functioning are central to genogram interpretation.

- Coincidences of dates: for example, the death of one family member or anniversary of this death occurring at the same time as symptom onset in another, or the age at symptom onset coinciding with the age of problem development of another family member.

- The impact of untimely life-cycle transitions: changes in functioning and relationships that correspond with critical family life events. Of particular interest are untimely life transitions: for example, births, marriages or deaths that occur 'off-schedule'.

Being aware of possible patterns makes the clinician more sensitive to what is missing. Such missing information about important family members or events and discrepancies in the information offered frequently reflect charged emotional issues in the family. The clinician should take careful note of the connections which family members make or fail to make with various events.

The purpose of the exercises below is to allow you to construct a temporal and emotional map of your own family. While constructing your genogram, pay particular attention to dates, anniversaries and major family markers such as births, deaths and moves. In addition, try to look for impact of concurring historical events upon your family such as wars, changes in economic and political movements or natural disasters.

EXERCISE |

(I) Using the symbols given in Figure 2.1, construct a genogram, paying particular attention to the significance of dates and relationship lines.

(J) Using a red pen, draw the line that signifies a close connection between family members who have a strong, positive relationship. For each case where you have done this, ask yourself why, and what evidence you have for this. Also ask yourself what each of the individuals you have identified would say about this: would they agree or disagree? In your own words describe what they would say about the individual in question.

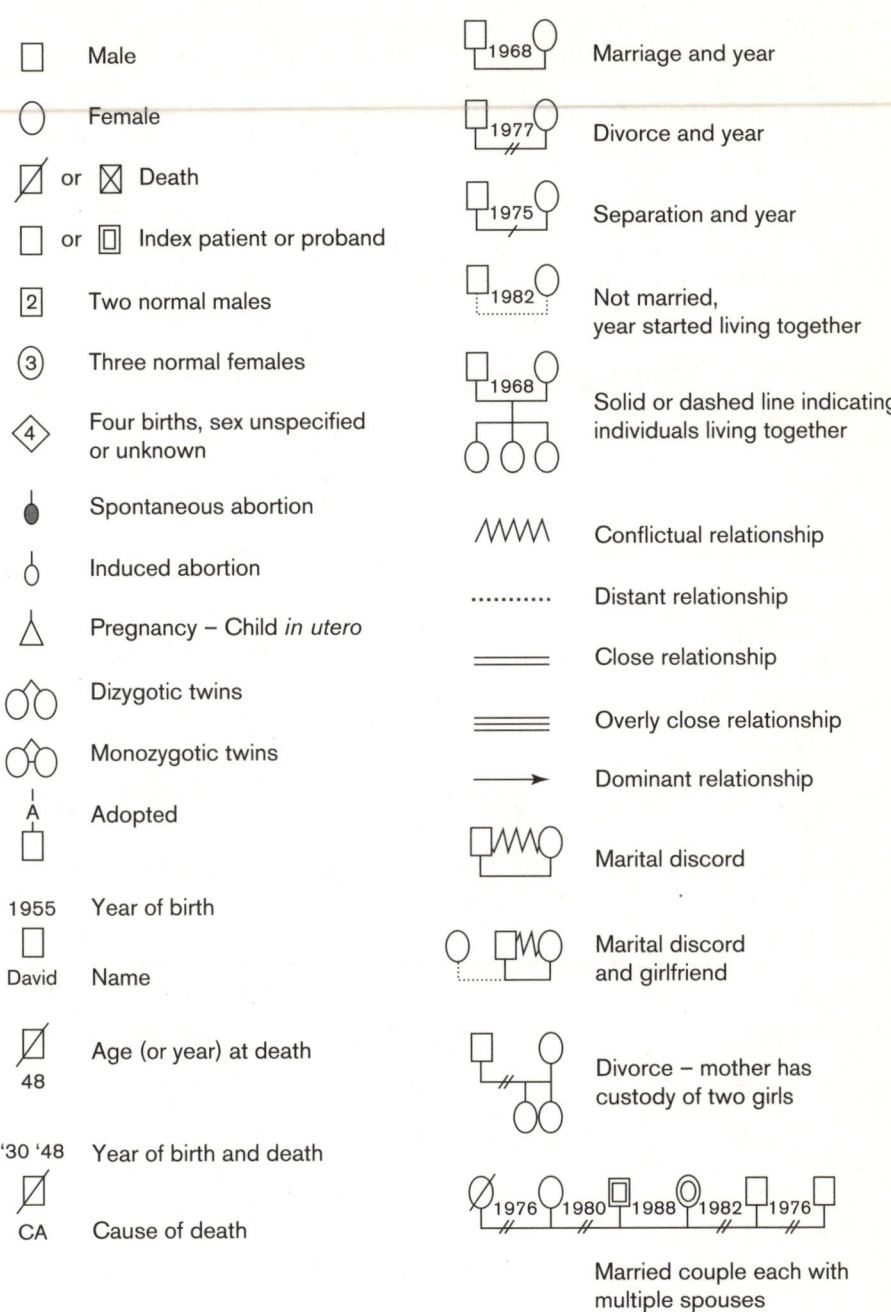

Figure 2.1 Symbols used in constructing a genogram

In order for an individual to move on to the next stage in the family life cycle (e.g. a parent facing an empty nest after children have left home) the family must reorganise itself at each pivotal point in the life cycle it enters (Rolland, 1984). These transitions can be difficult for some families, especially where there is a medical illness.

EXERCISE

(K) Can you see any ways that your genogram has emphasised relationships and events which you may not have considered so much in the past? What are these?

....

....

....

....

....

....

....

....

(L) Are there any pivotal points in your genogram? If so, what transitions did they affect and how difficult were these transitions?

....

....

....

....

....

....

....

....

(M) Now take yourself out of the genogram and reframe the genogram as you would imagine the relationships and events to differ in your absence (on an additional sheet). In what ways does this change the genogram? How has this process differed from the way you normally conceptualise the relationships between you and the important others around you?

....

....

....

....

....

....

....

....

Some trainee therapists may find the above exercises useful in order to reflect on why they may have been drawn into a professional caring role. Perhaps different events and relationship patterns have created a family dynamic that has helped to draw the trainee towards an aptitude or desire to care as a professional. It can be useful for supervision to be used as an instrument for the trainee to understand and explore their own response to the family.

Attention to process is vital in any family consultation, and Beck (1987) identifies five beneficial by-products of being process-orientated rather than approaching the construction of the genogram as an exercise in the application of techniques and interpretative categories. These by-products are: building or strengthening the therapeutic alliance, increased bonding of the family group, experience of re-creating the family dynamics in the session, client participation in the formulative phase of treatment, and an overall enhancement of the whole experience of this phase of family work.

The following is an example of the application and usefulness of genograms in counselling practice.

Case study: James and Clare

James and Clare Collins are a young couple living together, aged 29 and 25 years respectively, with two young children and a baby in utero (8 months). The couple came for counselling because Clare had become increasingly depressed and 'distant' over the previous two months. A counsellor suggested that, as a couple, they write down a family history in diagrammatic form.

From the genogram, James and Clare could be seen to have experienced a relatively high number of recent transitional life events and stresses in their family with regard to family members outside their immediate household. James' father's stroke had been a difficult time for the family and Clare said that she had started spending more time thinking about the loss of her own mother at around this point. She had increasingly missed her mother as her pregnancy developed and mourned the fact that her mother would never see her new grandchild. The loss had been particularly noticeable at this time because of her lack of other close female relatives from whom to seek support. Clare had not discussed this with James because she did not want to burden him with her concerns relating to a bereavement of three years earlier when he was worried about his father's health. James' parents were having marital difficulties and this, accompanied by Clare's sister's divorce, had made James and Clare particularly sensitive to conflicts and changes in their own relationship.

The counsellor was not able to fully exploit the value of constructing a genogram but covered some important areas in the time available in a comprehensible and focused way. The Collins were only booked in for one session and this session confirmed their view that Clare's depression and the couple's concern about their relationship was not solely attributable to hormonal changes or anxieties about the forthcoming baby. Discussion had been opened up in areas they both found difficult to talk about but which had been having a significant effect on the family. They opted to take their genogram away with them and undertook to continue the discussion at home, having already suggested a few possible ways forward in relation to some of their concerns.

EXERCISE |

As a practice exercise, construct a genogram of the above scenario on an additional sheet of paper.

CONCLUSIONS

The genogram is a valuable method for gathering family information. It provides counsellors with demographic and family information as well as medical data, both in the present and from the past. From the family's perspective, it provides a means for the explanation of family relationships and patterns. Genograms provide physicians with a diagnostic tool which takes into account the possible cause and effects of illness. From the counsellor's viewpoint, the family genogram is a means for personal exploration of the client's problem and a way of helping clients to understand and reframe their problems. From the perspective of a therapist in training, genograms can provide insights into patterns and pivotal experiences and to pinpoint the origins of values and beliefs that influence their own professional practice.

SUGGESTED FURTHER READING

Duck, S. (1998) *Human Relationships* (3rd edn). London: Sage.
Hargie, O.D.W. (ed) (1997) *The Handbook of Communication Skills* (2nd edn). London: Routledge.
McGoldrick, M. and Gerson, R. (eds) (1985) *Genograms in Family Assessment*. New York: Norton.

3

Culture

What does culture have to do with how I work as a therapist?

The term *culture* is generally used to refer to the customary beliefs, traits and social norms of racial, religious or social groups. In many ways our culture defines our boundaries and sets limits between our surroundings and ourselves. It allows us a sense of belonging, a collective 'specialness' that we take pride in and will fight and even make sacrifices for. However many aspects of culture are based on principles or doctrines that we are born into, that we never really question or challenge. Some are static and unchanging, others are dynamic and vary according to time and place; ultimately however, they serve to contribute to our definition of who we are and how we relate to those around us.

As individuals, it is important that we are able to examine how our culture has been integrated into our self-concept and how it affects our relationships with others. It is also important to look at our own *'isms'*, our overriding belief structures about cultures other than our own. To be effective both interpersonally and professionally we need to acknowledge and understand our own assumptions of human behaviour and recognise that those held by others may differ from our own.

As therapists, it is important that the counselling process is not impeded by cultural differences. Researchers have noted that in Western societies multi-cultural clients are more likely than white clients to have unfavourable experiences in counselling (Ridley, 1995). In particular, problems have been identified in terms of:

- *Diagnosis* – where minority clients tend to receive misdiagnosis overestimating the extent of psychopathology.
- *Type of treatment* – minority clients are more likely to receive medication only rather than medication and psychotherapy; they are also more likely to receive low-cost short-term treatments than are non-minority groups.
- *Treatment adherence* – minority clients have a significantly higher dropout rate from therapy than do non-minority groups.
- *Attitudes* – minority groups tend to report more dissatisfaction with psychological interventions and counselling in general.

(Gibson and Mitchell, 1999)

The following is a list of considerations for therapists working with clients from a different culture:

1. Identify expectations and beliefs about counselling.

2. Find out how the client feels about working with someone from a different culture.

3. Gather family information: norms of family interaction/make-up may be different for other cultures.

4. Keep in mind that stigma against mental illness exists within many cultures; as such, restraint should be exercised when gathering information.

5. Help clients develop their own goals for therapy. This will help to ensure that the world view of the therapist is not imposed upon the client.

   In order to explore the above issues, open questions such as 'How do you feel about coming to see a counsellor?' and ' What would you like to get from these sessions?' could be used. In order to explore cultural issues concerning the client and counselling, open questions such as 'How do you feel about working in these sessions with a counsellor from a different cultural background?' can be used to understand the client's perspective. Genograms (which are expanded upon in Chapter 2) will help the counsellor to obtain a further understanding of family relationships.

EXERCISE |

List below a few open-ended questions you could use to elicit information pertaining to the list of do's above:

....

....

....

....

....

....

....

List below a suitable list of don't's with respect to multicultural counselling:

....

....

....

....

....

....

....

Investigating your own cultural assumptions

Describe yourself culturally:

....

....

....

....

....

What does culture mean to you?

....

....

....

....

....

....

What traits do you associate with the following religious or spiritual philosophies?

Christianity ....

Roman Catholic ....

Judaism ....

Islam ....

Buddhism ....

CULTURAL INTERPRETATION OF BEHAVIOUR

Kleinman (1988), a medical anthropologist, puts forward the idea that the health-, illness- and healthcare-related aspects of societies are expressed as cultural systems. He believes that healthcare systems should be viewed as other cultural symbolic systems, such as kinship and religion, which are built out of meanings, values and behavioural norms.

Emotional behaviour needs to be understood in the client's cultural context, with a consciousness of the dominant Eurocentric viewpoint. A relevant example to consider here would be the number of people of Afro-Caribbean descent admitted into British psychiatric hospitals in recent years suffering from schizophrenia – which outweigh white British admissions by three to one. Why should this be? Are Afro-Caribbeans more prone to schizophrenia? Or is mental distress, due to many extremely difficult social factors, being interpreted as schizophrenia?

Gaines (1982) suggests that the patient, the family and their culture, as well as that of the practitioner, need to be explained and understood, and that each is an equally important ingredient of the cultural construction of illness and treatment.

An example of the interpretation of behaviour in the therapeutic context is the view taken of eye contact between therapist and client. In many Western therapeutic models this contact is considered essential to the relationship, and avoidance of it is thought to be therapeutically significant. For many traditional Asian clients direct eye contact might be considered disrespectful, or, in the case of women, immodest. An Indian psychiatrist tells of being summoned to a hospital by a white colleague who was unable to proceed with an Indian client because of the lack of eye contact.

What other issues might arise as part of the therapeutic process that could perhaps cause problems due to cultural differences?

....

....

....

....

....

What action might you be able to take to address these issues?

....

....

....

....

....

We, as therapists, need to consider our own limitations, who we are as people, what we represent, and the prejudices and biases we bring to the relationship, in order that we may learn not to impose our own cultural values. We could call this a respect of difference. The acknowledgement and handling of differences can be very threatening, and it is often managed by denial and an attempt to make everyone the same. In intercultural work our aim is to encourage counsellors and therapists to think and talk about these issues, and perhaps to look at and work on our own prejudices.

EXERCISE |

A white British counsellor was unsure of what to do when a Nigerian client brought her a gift. Should she have refused it categorically as seduction as her training had taught her, or should this gesture be viewed in the client's cultural context?

What would you do in this situation and why?

....

....

....

....

....

Thinking candidly about yourself, what assumptions and biases do you
think you may bring to the therapeutic process?

....

....

....

....

....

What effect might these assumptions and biases have on the therapeutic
process both with European and non-European clients?

....

....

....

....

....

Jafar Kareem (Kareem and Littlewood, 1992) asks the question: 'What does it
mean to communicate across cultures?' He states that there are racial differences
in 'cultural' attributes such as concepts of personhood, respect or disrespect,
independence, position of elders in the family, obligations to family and community
– the very notion of moral conditions that combine to make a person a social being
rather than an isolated organism. He believes that an understanding of these
aspects of human life is fundamental to the success of any therapy. The need for
psychotherapists and counsellors to take such matters into consideration both in
their practice and training is now widely acknowledged.

THE IMPACT OF RACISM

Addressing the impact of racism forms another essential ingredient of intercultural
therapy – acknowledging and working with the pain and the emotional damage it
causes. Racism is an emotional and highly charged issue and there are no simple

solutions. Living in a white host society, black and other ethnic minorities often receive the racist message, whether consciously or unconsciously, that they are inferior. As therapists, we need to take on this knowledge as central to the issue of racism – we also need to look at the ingredients of racism which constitute basic feelings of envy, hate, jealousy, greed, competitiveness, anger, violence, suspicion, fear and ignorance – feelings we all have inside us. That is perhaps why racism is so threatening.

EXERCISES |

Where does your family originate?

....

Think of the last time you were in a foreign country: what was different, what was the same? Were expressions of emotion different? If so, how?

....

....

....

....

....

Look at the randomly selected list of countries below and pick a word that you feel describes each group collectively:

England ....
France ....
Germany ....
India ....
Pakistan ....
Japan ....
China ....
Ethiopia ....
South Africa ....

Write down why you chose the words above. Is it based on a single incident? An encounter? Reading? Travelling?

....

....

....

....

....

Now imagine being described by the words that you have used to describe the cultures: How do you feel? Do you feel that any of the words you used to describe the other cultures apply to you? What word do you think most adequately describes your cultural group?

....

....

....

....

....

Think of a time when you felt that you were the object of discrimination due to your cultural beliefs or values. Describe the incident below:

....

....

....

....

....

....

Now check what you have written and list the words you used to describe the way you were feeling.

....

....

....

....

....

Insert each word into the sentence below next to the asterix and complete the sentence:

I was feeling *_____ because

....

....

I was feeling *_____ because

....

....

I was feeling *_____ because

....

....

I was feeling *_____ because

....

....

List the words you used to describe the other person involved in the incident.

....

....

....

....

....

....

Were these exercises uncomfortable? If they were, this is probably because it is difficult to sum up a culture in a word; it does not do justice to the individual or the group as a whole. The intention of this exercise was to underscore the fact that cultural diversity exists within defined cultures, and, as such, gross generalisations regarding these issues are often inaccurate and insulting.

In working with the effects of racism, an intercultural therapy approach is that emotional distress is not always seen as self-induced but can be caused by external factors, and we aim to look at the effect of the social factors on the inner psyche. Our work encompasses the inner experiences of the client, together with their total life experience – including their communal experience and life before their arrival on Western soil. Mr J. had been a headmaster of a flourishing school in South Africa and a respected member of his community before he emigrated to Britain so that his family could escape the degradation of being black in the apartheid system. Forced to take on both a day and evening job to cover the high costs of living in London with a large family, Mr J. eventually sought help for depression and chronic illness.

Intercultural therapy enhances existing practices of therapy. It is based on the relationship between the client and the therapist, and in this relationship we emphasise acknowledging and working with difference. Kareem and Littlewood (1992) cite the example of Victoria who, when consulting a white woman therapist because she had become depressed and feared that she was going mad, was made to feel that issues of race were essentially her problem. Whenever she tried to bring up anything relating to her feelings about being black, the therapist always interpreted this as a projection of her inner chaos into the outside world. Victoria felt misunderstood and angry that her pain and confusion about being in a black/white situation where she was made to feel powerless went unacknowledged. She finally sought help from the Nafsiyat Therapy Centre because she needed a therapist who could immediately recognise her pain in being powerless and black in a racist society. The problem with the first therapist was not that she was white, but that she was unable to look at the interrelated themes of race and powerlessness as problems of reality.

Psychotherapy and counselling have until recently often been a white middle-class perogative, largely for economic reasons, but perhaps also because black and other ethnic minority people were thought of as psychologically unsuitable. We are now breaking through these social boundaries, both in theory and practice, and stress the need for practitioners to confront their own limitations, and to look at what they might be unconsciously projecting on to ethnic minority clients.

Interestingly, Kareem and Littlewood (1992) suggest that there is a double-edged argument going on between minority groups and white psychotherapists, with a great deal of hostility towards counselling and psychotherapy from the former because it is seen as essentially a 'Western, middle-class' form of treatment.

EXERCISE |

What forms of cultural-based hostility have you or might you encounter as a therapist?

....

....

....

....

....

....

Why do you think this is so, and what do you think is the most effective way to address the issue?

....

....

....

....

....

....

One of the major reasons for the distrust expressed by black and ethnic minority clients is the inevitable imbalance of power that exists between therapist and client. This imbalance is a mirror image of the experience of powerlessness that black and ethnic minority clients feel in daily life situations, and they do not want the same situation to operate in a therapeutic encounter. This experience of powerlessness, especially for black clients, is a potent element in the therapeutic situation and one that must be addressed if work is to proceed.

The idea of intercultural therapy is to make the psychotherapeutic healing process available to black and ethnic minorities – to expand the limitations of the field. Its essence is in its inherent humanity, the respect for each other in our difference, whether in language, history or traditions, and this approach enlarges our understanding of human experience.

CHALLENGING YOUR OWN CULTURAL ASSUMPTIONS

Effective therapists utilise core principles when working with their multicultural clients but at the same time respect the uniqueness and individuality of each client they see. It is imperative to acknowledge that every client needs to be approached and understood from their unique frame of reference and as such normative rules do not always apply to individual clients.

(Gibson and Mitchell, 1999)

Part of the process of becoming an effective counsellor involves learning how to recognise diversity, and shaping your counselling practice to fit the client's world. It is essential for counsellors to develop sensitivity to cultural differences if they hope to make interventions that are congruent with the values of their clients. Counsellors bring their own cultural beliefs and values with them to their work, so they must know how cultural conditioning has influenced the directions they take with their clients. Moreover, unless the social and cultural context of clients is taken into consideration, it is very difficult to appreciate the nature of their struggles. Many counselling students have come to value characteristics such as making their own choices, expressing what they are feeling, being open and self-revealing and striving for independence, yet some of their clients may not share these goals. Certain cultures emphasise being emotionally reserved or being selective about sharing personal concerns. Counsellors need to determine whether the assumptions they have made about the nature and functioning of therapy are appropriate for culturally diverse populations.

Clearly, effective counselling must take into account the impact of culture. Since culture is quite simply the values and behaviours shared by a group of people, we should understand that culture does not refer only to an ethnic or racial heritage but includes age, gender, religion, lifestyle, physical and mental ability and socioeconomic status. Counsellors have two choices: to ignore the influence of culture or attend to it. Whatever choice is made, culture will continue to influence both the client's and the counsellor's behaviour, with or without the counsellor's awareness.

Effective counsellors understand their own cultural conditioning, the conditioning of their clients and the sociopolitical system of which they are a part. Acquiring this understanding begins with counsellors' awareness of any cultural values, biases and attitudes that may hinder their development of a positive view of pluralism. Sue *et al.* (1992) have developed a conceptual framework for competencies and standards in multicultural counselling. Their dimensions of competency involve three areas: beliefs and attitudes, knowledge and skill.

BELIEFS AND ATTITUDES OF CULTURALLY SKILLED COUNSELLORS

First, effective counsellors have moved from being culturally unaware to ensuring that their personal biases, values or problems will not interfere with their ability to work with clients who are culturally different to them. They do not allow their fear of discovering or owning up to their prejudices to block them from a multicultural perspective. They seek to examine and understand the world from the vantage point of their clients. They respect clients' religious and spiritual beliefs and values. They are comfortable with differences between themselves and others in terms of race, ethnicity, culture and beliefs. Because these therapists welcome diverse value orientations and assumptions about human behaviour, they have a basis for sharing the world view of their clients as opposed to being culturally encapsulated. They value bilingualism and do not view another language as an impediment to counselling.

KNOWLEDGE OF CULTURALLY SKILLED COUNSELLORS

Second, culturally effective practitioners possess certain knowledge. They know specifically about their own racial and cultural heritage and how it affects them personally. Because they understand the dynamics of oppression, racism, discrimination and stereotyping, they are in a position to detect their own racist attitudes, beliefs and feelings. They understand the world view of their clients and they learn about their clients' cultural backgrounds. Because they understand the basic values underlying the therapeutic process, they know how these values may clash with the cultural values of some minority groups. They understand that external sociopolitical forces influence all groups, and they know these forces operate with respect to the treatment of minorities. These practitioners are aware of the institutional barriers that prevent minorities from utilising the mental health services available in their community. They possess knowledge about the historical background, traditions and values of the client populations with whom they are working. They know about minority family structures, hierarchies, values and beliefs. Furthermore, they are knowledgeable about community characteristics and resources. Culturally skilled counsellors know how to help clients make use of indigenous resources where appropriate. In areas where they are lacking knowledge, they seek resources to assist them. The greater their depth and breadth of knowledge of culturally diverse groups, the more likely they are to be effective practitioners.

SKILLS AND INTERVENTION STRATEGIES OF CULTURALLY SKILLED COUNSELLORS

Third, effective counsellors have acquired certain skills in working with culturally diverse populations. Multicultural counselling is enhanced when practitioners use methods and strategies, and define goals consistent with the life experiences and cultural values of their clients. Such practitioners modify and adapt their interventions so as to accommodate cultural differences. They do not force their clients to fit within one counselling approach. They are able to send and receive both verbal and non-verbal messages accurately and appropriately. They are willing to seek out educational, consultative and training experiences to enhance their ability to work with culturally diverse client populations.

INCORPORATING CULTURE INTO COUNSELLING PRACTICE

Although practitioners can acquire general knowledge and skills that will enable them to function effectively with diverse client populations, it is not realistic to expect that they will know everything about the cultural background of a client. There is much to be said about letting clients teach counsellors about the relevant aspects of their culture. It is a good idea for counsellors to ask clients to provide them with the information they will need to work effectively. It helps to assess the degree of acculturation and identity development that has taken place. This is especially true for individuals who have the experience of living in more than one culture. They often have allegiance to their own culture and yet they may find certain characteristics of their new culture attractive. They may experience conflicts in integrating the two cultures in which they live. These core struggles can be productively explored in the therapeutic context if the counsellor understands and respects this cultural conflict.

WELCOMING DIVERSITY

Counselling is by its very nature diverse in the context of a multicultural society, so it is easy to see why there are no ideal therapeutic approaches. Instead, different theories have distinct features that hold appeal for different cultural groups. There are also distinct limitations of some theoretical approaches when applied to certain populations.

EXERCISE

Write down some limitations of theoretical approaches that you can think of when they are applied to certain populations.

....

....

....

....

....

....

....

....

For what reasons do you think these limitations apply to these populations?

....

....

....

....

....

Effective multicultural counselling requires an open stance on the part of the practitioner, flexibility, and a willingness to modify strategies to fit the needs and the situation of the individual client. Practitioners who truly respect their clients will be aware of a client's hesitation and will not be too quick to misinterpret this behaviour. Instead, they will patiently wait to enter the world of their client as far as they are able. It is not necessary for practitioners to have the same experiences as their clients; what is more important is that they attempt to be open to a similar set of feelings and struggles. It is not always by similarity but rather by differences that we are challenged to look at what we are doing.

Reflecting on the following guidelines and questions may increase your effectiveness in serving diverse client populations.

EXERCISE |

- Learn more about the ways in which your own cultural background has an influence on your thinking and behaving. What specific steps can you take to broaden your base of understanding, both of your own and other cultures?

....

....

....

....

....

- Identify your basic assumptions – especially as they apply to diversity in culture, ethnicity, race, gender, class, religion and lifestyle – and think: How are your assumptions likely to affect your practice as a counsellor?

....

....

....

....

....

- Where did you obtain your knowledge about culture?

....

....

....

....

....

....

- Are your attitudes about diverse cultures your own and have you carefully examined them?

....

....

....

....

....

- Learn to pay attention to the common ground that exists between people of different backgrounds. What are some of the ways in which we all share universal concerns?

....

....

....

....

....

- Realise that it is not necessary to learn everything about the cultural backgrounds of your clients before you begin working with them. Allow them to teach you how you can best serve them.
- Spend time preparing clients for counselling. Teach them how to use their therapeutic experience to meet the challenges they face in their everyday lives.
- Recognise the importance of being flexible in applying the methods you use with clients. Don't be wedded to a specific technique if it is not appropriate for a given client.

- Remember that practising from a multicultural perspective can make your job easier, and can be rewarding for both you and your clients.

CRITIQUES OF EXISTING APPROACHES

Critiques of existing multicultural approaches are developing apace. One of these relates to the assumptions underlying various approaches. As discussed, seminal texts in the area of improving intercultural competence emphasise the need for increased sensitivity or awareness on the part of the counsellor (e.g. Sue and Sue, 1990) as a prerequisite for effective practice. The underlying assumption is that such sensitivity and awareness will automatically improve counselling effectiveness. Ridley (1995) questions this, arguing that the concept has not yet been satisfactorily defined, concise guidelines on how to operationalise the concept have not yet been developed and the means to measure whether it has been achieved do not yet exist. The contention is that 'these flaws are fatal because they hamper application of the construct, destroying its usefulness for multicultural counselling, training and research.' Harway (1979) however, writing from a feminist perspective, suggested a set of revisions to existing counsellor training courses to make them more responsible to the needs of women. McLeod (1998) believes that this model is just as appropriate as a way of promoting awareness of the 'needs' of other minority or disadvantaged client groups. The principal tenets of this 'cultural training' model are described below. Comment on how useful you would find these tenets to training and why you would or would not advocate their use.

EXERCISE |

- Employ a significant proportion of 'minority' staff.

....

....

....

....

....

- Enrol a significant proportion of 'minority' students.

....

....

....

....

....

- Encourage research on topics relevant to counselling with disadvantaged groups.

....

....

....

....

....

- Provide library resources in these areas.

....

....

....

....

....

- Require experiential sessions both for staff and students to facilitate examination of attitudes and stereotypes.

....

....

....

....

....

- Encourage staff to use culturally aware language and teaching materials.

....

....

....

....

....

Other critiques are concerned with the potentially diluting effect of multiculturalism as an approach embracing too many social differences. Richardson and Helms (1994) argue that:

> Whereas multiculturalism may be a useful construct for encouraging discussion about matters of culture in society in general, it is virtually useless as a scientific construct. In particular, the lack of specificity about which aspects of individual diversity are appropriately subsumed under the rubric of multiculturalism has contributed to considerable confusion in theory, research and practice.

If this dilution is to be halted, more rigour must be applied in the use of cultural – in particular racial – constructs. It has been argued that the recognition of cultural difference and increased sensitivity does not address the 'exploitative and oppressive power relations endemic within white society' and that a much more radical approach is required to 'anti-racism', focusing more on an understanding of power relationships within society.

CONCLUSION

Each culture has its own approach to understanding and supporting people who have emotional and psychological problems. Counsellors can draw upon these resources, such as traditional healers, religious groups and social networks, when working with clients. The possibility of integrating indigenous and Western counselling approaches, to create a mode of help that is tailored to meet the needs of a specific client group, offers great promise as a means of extending and renewing the practice and profession of counselling.

It is important to realise that it takes time, study and experience to become an effective multicultural counsellor. Multicultural competence cannot be reduced simply to cultural awareness and sensitivity, to a body of knowledge, or to a specific set of skills. This multicultural expertise requires that counsellors have sufficient breadth and depth in all areas (Leong and Kim, 1991).

SUGGESTED FURTHER READING

Davis, L.E., Enola, E. and Proctor, K. (1995) *Race, Gender and Class: Guidelines for Practice with Individuals, Families, and Groups.* London: Prentice Hall.

Gibson, R.L. and Mitchell, M.H. (1999) *Introduction to Counselling and Guidance*. London: Prentice Hall.

Kareem, J. and Littlewood, R. (eds) (1992) *Intercultural Therapy – Themes, Interpretations and Practice*. Oxford: Blackwell Scientific.

Kleinman, A. (1988) *The Illness Narratives: Suffering Healing and the Human Condition*. New York: Basic Books.

Richardson, T. and Helms, J.E. (1994) The relationship of the racial identity attitudes of black men to perceptions of 'parallel' counselling dyads. *Journal of Counselling and Development*, 73, 2, 172–177.

Ridley, C.R. (1995) *Overcoming Unintentional Racism in Counselling and Psychotherapy*. Thousand Oaks. CA: Sage.

Sue, D. W. and Sue, D. (1990). *Counselling the Culturally Different* (2nd edn). Chichester: Wiley.

Gender

What does it mean to you to be male or female, and, perhaps more importantly, what are the implications of these meanings?

The implications of personal, social and political meanings attached to gender have ramifications for who you are and how you live. They also have profound implications for how you conduct the specific business of working therapeutically with others. We have constructed a range of exercises that we hope will help you to experientially answer the questions central to this chapter. Before you move on it is important to ensure that we are using words consistently. Below are some terms separated from their definition. As an introductory task, place one of the following words by the definition that seems most appropriate: sexuality, androgyny, sexual abuse, sex, masculine, feminine, transsexual, gender.

_____ whether one is born biologically female or male (Albino Gilbert and Scher, 1999, p.3).

_____ expression of the attempt to discharge energy from sexual drives and often measured in terms of the desire for intimacy, eroticism and sexual activity (Albino Gilbert and Scher, 1999).

_____ psychological, social and cultural features and characteristics that have become strongly associated with the biological categories of male and female (Albino Gilbert and Scher, 1999, p.3).

_____ the possession of both 'instrumental' personality characteristics (often associated with traditional notions of 'masculinity') and 'expressive' personality characteristics (often associated with traditional notions of 'femininity') (Bem, 1993).

_____ psychological, social and cultural features and characteristics that have become strongly associated with the biological category of male (Albino Gilbert and Scher, 1999).

_____ psychological, social and cultural features and characteristics that have become strongly associated with the biological category of female (Albino Gilbert and Scher, 1999).

_____ when someone less powerful or informed is persuaded or coerced to engage in activities that are initiated to meet the sexual drives of another.

_____ desire to change one's genitals and secondary sex characteristics and adopt a gendered lifestyle associated with the opposite sex.

In forming a personal answer to the question, 'What impact does my gender have on shaping who I am?', it may be helpful to think about who you are as the sum total of the way you experience yourself and the world. It involves anticipating, thinking, feeling and being. It is reflected in your experience, and at times it may manifest in terms of joy, sexual drive, frustration, amusement and confusion.

EXERCISE |

Identity is constructed both personally and in relation to others. How do others know you are male or female? Answer this question by anticipating the perspectives of a range of others: of those who are intimately familiar with you, those who may work alongside you, or those who may casually notice you in the street. In answering this question it is important not to speak in terms of generalities. Be as specific as possible, citing evidence for your view.

....

....

....

....

....

....

....

....

....

....

As a child, do you ever recall being mistaken for someone of the opposite sex? Write what you recall from this experience, paying particular attention to your bodily reaction. Were you embarrassed, did you correct the other person or did you remain silent in order to avoid embarrassing them for their mistake?

....

....

....

....

....

....

....

....

In view of what you have written above, how do you imagine you would feel if this happened today? Do you anticipate that you would feel differently? If so, why?

....

....

....

....

....

....

....

....

Draw a picture of a girl and a boy as you would if you were 5 years old. You may find it easier if you use your non-preferred hand to hold the pencil, and try not to be concerned about the quality or realism of your drawing.

What do you notice about your picture? What are the stereotypical indicators of sex that you have included in your illustration? Make a list of at least six definitive features below.

1. ....

2. ....

3. ....

4. ....

5. ....

6. ....

They may seem silly to you now, but, back then, did you experience them as real? If so, do you recall when you began to question the definitive and absolute nature of these qualities?

SENTENCE COMPLETION

The following exercise is designed to get you to begin to think about the impact of sex on your personal perspectives, relationships and life choices. Don't spend too much time thinking about your response. Write the first thing that comes into your head.

EXERCISE |

If I were *[of the opposite sex]* I would spend a lot more time........

....

....

Because I am *[of my sex]* I think about . . .

....

....

If I were of the opposite sex I would be different because . . .

....

....

As I have grown older my views about masculinity, femininity and androgyny have changed . . .

....

....

The clothes I wear are similar to those worn by people of the same sex as me in that they . . .

....

....

If I were of the opposite sex my relationship with my . . . [from the list below] . . . would be different because . . .

Mother ....

Father ....

Sister ....

Brother ....

Lover ....

Best friend ....

Difficult work colleague ....

Review and reflect on what you have written above. Are you surprised by anything that you have written? Complete the following sentence as a way of reaching some closure regarding the content of this exercise.

My view of sex and its relationship to gender will be helpful in the execution of the role of counsellor because . . .

....

....

....

....

....

The aim of the exercises presented in this chapter have been to focus your awareness on both the abstruse and obvious implications of growing up and living in a society that makes much of the biological sex to which you are born. Each of us experiences those aspects of self, understood under the rubric of sex, uniquely. Having sensitised yourself to your current and historical experience of sex it is now time to turn your attention to the implications of your unique perspective on this topic for therapeutic practice. Making global assumptions about the profound implications of sex and its relationship to gendered experience can be as naive and disruptive to the therapeutic process as acting as if sex and gender were irrelevant. Rather than just accepting this statement, it might be worthwhile identifying why and how a therapist's view of gender can influence practice.

It is critically important to take your client seriously, recognising the weight of their experience. As therapists, we have the capacity to implicitly and explicitly validate the viability or 'truth' of our clients' constructions of the implications of sex and their relationship to gender. The following case study provides a context within which such issues can be explored. As you read and reflect on the case, imagine you are the therapist. Some questions follow the account.

Case study: Thomas

Thomas is a 46-year-old transsexual who was referred to you by his GP with depression and suicidal ideation. In the referral letter the GP outlined Thomas' domestic circumstances in which he described him as a quiet man, married to his present wife for twenty-two years. He further informed you that he has two children, a son aged 16 and a daughter aged 20. From the GP's account it would appear that Thomas' family are generally supportive of his attempts to live with his transsexual identity.

Thomas presents as distinctively tall and awkward, solid in statue, with a long, angular face accentuated by a strong, square jaw. On meeting for the first time you were struck by his unconvincing appearance as a woman and you recall feeling uncomfortable as he repeatedly sought validation for his 'feminine appearance'.

On interview you learn from your client that he recently left his long-term place of employment as he felt he was unsupported and ostracised by colleagues following his presentation at a staff social event wearing women's clothing. He reports feeling unhappy at home despite what he sees as his family's significant efforts to support and accommodate his lifestyle choice. He says he feels that this support may change if he was to tell his wife and children of his desire to pursue gender reassignment surgery and ultimately meet and marry a man he loved.

Thomas said that he had been managing pretty well until he was referred for, but refused, gender reassignment surgery at an NHS hospital. Since that time he reported that he did not think he could cope, and saw no way forward. In your second session with Thomas he informs you that he has appealed against the decision of the hospital to refuse him the operation. In order to bolster his appeal he requires you to write to the admitting surgeon informing him that, in your view, if he is not granted the surgery, he will almost certainly commit suicide. Subsequent to this session you receive a telephone call from his wife in which she asks you directly what the chances are of keeping her husband and saving her marriage. As you listen, you are struck by the warmth, compassion and depth of feeling she has for her husband.

What thoughts and feelings occur to you as you read this case? Did you experience any tension between what you 'should' feel and think, and what you did feel and think? Imagine that you have only one final chance to speak to Thomas, who has directly asked you what you think about his situation and what he should do.

In the space below you should write three replies to Thomas: one from the perspective of a therapist, one from the perspective of his wife, and one from the perspective of the 'average person in the street'.

Thomas: What should I do?

Therapist's response:

....

....

....

....

....

Wife's response:

....

....

....

....

....

Average person in the street's response:

....

....

....

....

....

On reflection of what you have written above, do you see any areas of contrast and overlap? What makes the various perspectives similar or different? Do you see any or all of these perspectives reflecting aspects of your own personal view of Thomas' case?

When we think about and describe ourselves sexually we have no option but to draw upon culturally constructed categories (Burr and Butt, 1996). This is often an automatic and unconscious process. Through the use of the following exercises we would like you to reflect on your understanding of your sexual

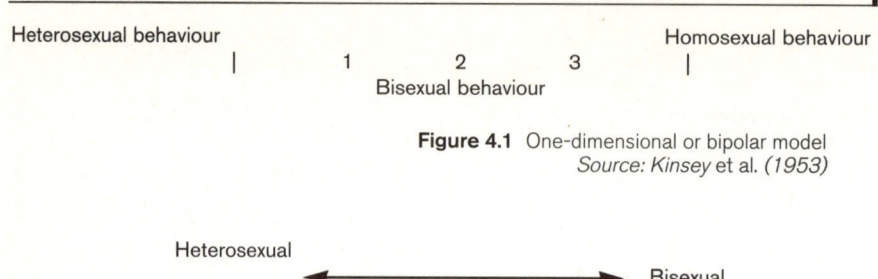

Figure 4.1 One-dimensional or bipolar model
Source: Kinsey et al. (1953)

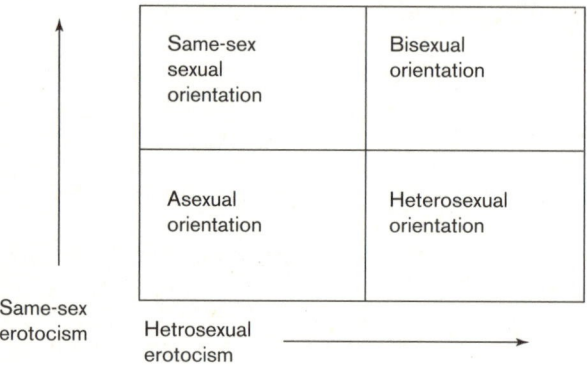

Figure 4.2 Ross and Paul model
Source: Ross and Paul (1992)

Same-sex sexual orientation	Bisexual orientation
Asexual orientation	Heterosexual orientation

Same-sex erotocism

Hetrosexual erotocism

Figure 4.3 Two-dimensional model
Source: Storms (1981)

orientation. By sexual orientation we are thinking of the unique and personal influences of sexual desire. These are the elements of attraction and the things that gain your sexual attention. One of the most common and popularly agreed upon constructions of sexual orientation is the homosexual versus heterosexual dimension.

Below we have laid out several competing conceptualisations of sexual orientation (Figures 4.1–4.3). We would like you to reflect upon each and ask yourself which you believe most accurately represents human sexuality. In the one-dimensional or bipolar model, sexual behaviour is seen as a continuum with heterosexuality and homosexuality at its extremes. The Ross and Paul model (1992) places homosexual and heterosexual at the same pole of a continuum and bisexuality at the opposite, on the basis that homosexuals and heterosexuals share an attraction based on the sex of their partner. This model asserts that bisexuals may emphasise features such as personality and social characteristics to inform their choice of desired sexual partner.

The two dimensions of gender and eroticism are combined in the Storms (1981) model and result in the conceptualisation of sexual orientation into four quadrants: asexual orientation, same-sex sexual orientation, bisexual orientation and heterosexual orientation.

In order to assist you in exploring issues of sex and gender, a brief questionnaire adapted from Coleman (1990) is provided for you to complete. This inventory may provide surprising insights now or fascinating evidence of growth and change when you review your responses in the future.

Sexual self checklist
What is your current relationship status?

☐   Single; no sexual partner

☐   Single; one regular sexual partner

☐   Single; multiple sexual partners

☐   Coupled; living together (exclusive sexual relationship)

☐   Coupled; living together (open sexual relationship)

☐   Coupled; living apart (exclusive sexual relationship)

☐   Coupled; living apart (open sexual relationship)

☐   Other (specify) _____

In terms of my *current* sexual orientation I see myself as . . .

☐   Exclusively lesbian/gay

☐   Predominantly lesbian/gay

☐   Bisexual

☐   Predominantly heterosexual

☐   Exclusively heterosexual

☐   Other (specify) _____

In terms of my sexual orientation in the *future* see myself as . . .

☐   Exclusively lesbian/gay

☐   Predominantly lesbian/gay

☐   Bisexual

☐   Predominantly heterosexual

☐   Exclusively heterosexual

☐   Other (specify) _____

In terms of my current sexual orientation I see my self as . . .

Very comfortable | | | | | Very uncomfortable

Physical identity

I was born as a biological . . .

Male | | | | | | | | Female

Ideally, I wish I had been born . . .

Male | | | | | | | | Female

Gender identity

I think of myself physically as . . .

Male | | | | | | | | Female

Ideally I would like to think of myself as . . .

Male | | | | | | | | Female

In my sexual fantasies I imagine myself physically as . . .

Male | | | | | | | | Female

In my future sexual fantasies I would like to imagine myself physically as . . .

Male | | | | | | | | Female

Sex-role Identity

My interests, attitudes, appearance and behaviour would be considered to be
female or male (as traditionally defined) . . .

Male | | | | | | | | Female

I wish my interests, attitudes, appearance, and behaviours were considered to be
female or male (as traditionally defined) . . .

Male | | | | | | | | Female

Sexual orientation identity

My sexual behaviour has been with . . .

Male | | | | | | | | Female

I wish my sexual behaviour had been with . . .

Male | | | | | | | | Female

My sexual fantasies have been with . . .

Male | | | | | | | | Female

I wish my sexual fantasies would be with . . .

Male | | | | | | | | Female

My emotional attachments have been with . . .

Male | | | | | | | | Female

I wish my emotional attachments would be with . . .

Male | | | | | | | | Female

Reflect on what you have written above. Do you imagine you would have completed this checklist differently one, two, five or ten years ago?

Clients may infer our capacity to understand perspectives on sensitive topics on the basis of any gendered messages that we convey. The expression of gender stereotypes can occur outside of our awareness. Engaging in exercises such as those given throughout this chapter will help us identify what beliefs and behaviours, if expressed, are likely to send messages to our clients regarding our stance on the relationship between sex and gender. Even where we are careful not to validate stereotypes, clients are still free to make assumptions about us based on our biological sex. At the very least, with increased self-awareness, we can be clearer as to whether the assumptions expressed in therapy have more to do with our clients' beliefs than our behaviour.

SUGGESTED FURTHER READING

Golombok, S. and Fivush, R. (1994) *Gender Development*. Cambridge: Cambridge University Press.

Pope-Davis, D.B. and Coleman, H.L.K. (2001) *The Intersection of Race, Class, and Gender in Multicultural Counseling*. London: Sage.

Walkerdine, V. (1989) *Counting Girls Out*. London: Virago.

5

Ethics

What is the relationship between my personal morals, values and professional ethics?

Ethics are complex, and have far-reaching implications for the practice of counselling, counselling psychology and psychotherapy. It would be ambitious, foolish and misleading to set out to provide you with ready-made solutions to the ethical issues that may confront you. Ethical dilemmas by their definition are not amenable to manualarised resolution. Rather here we set ourselves the task of making explicit a range of principles that have been asserted to underlie ethical practice and examine the fit between these principles and your own value and moral position.

BACKGROUND

The beginning of philosophical ethics has often been linked to Socrates (*c*.470–399 BC). There seems little doubt for some that the example of Socrates, as represented in the writings of Plato (430–347 BC), helped to establish moral philosophy as a distinct subject. 'Ethics' comes from the Greek *ethos*, meaning character, and 'morality' from the Latin *mores*, which refers to custom and habit. Recent history has often seen the two words used interchangeably, or with rather uncertain differences. More recently, arguments have been put forward to sharpen the distinction. Ethics is a broader notion and includes much that would fall outside of that described as pertaining to morality (Becker and Becker, 1992).

Both morals and ethics often share common subject matter, with their respective concerns frequently overlapping. It may be that the difficulties inherent in distinguishing morality and ethics has led both to a preponderance of definitions based on what they are not, rather than a focus on what constitutes each domain of knowledge. Although difficult to define, it is possible to identify characteristics of morality that are seen as outside the remit of a number of ethical theories. Three characteristics of morality include: (1) a strict demand for responsibility (e.g., where 'ought' implies 'can' and 'should' implies 'will'), (2) the prominence of *duty* or *obligation* as the basic moral notion, (3) an essential concern for the non-instrumental good of others (Becker and Becker, 1992).

Values constitute an acknowledgement that some features of things are important to take into account in decision-making or when confronted with a choice. Those who see values as 'subjective' think of this in terms of a 'personal stance', a choice immune from rational argument (Blackburn, 1996). Values, although personal, may be seen as imbued from an external referent and thus deemed by some to be 'objective'. Objective values are those where choice can be guided by an independent standpoint such as rationality, God, authority or standards of ethical practice (Blackburn, 1996). Ethical practice therefore becomes both a personal stance and a professional requirement.

EXERCISE

What values influenced your choice to pursue a career in therapy and where did they originate from?

....

....

....

....

....

....

....

ETHICS IN THE PRACTICE OF COUNSELLING COUNSELLING PSYCHOLOGY AND PSYCHOTHERAPY

Welfel and Kitchener (1992) draw our attention to what they see as five of the basic principles underscoring ethical codes. These principles have been discussed and adapted by a range of authors including Corey (1996) who sees working to the benefit of clients, doing no harm, respecting others' autonomy and being fair and faithful as basic to professional therapeutic practice. These principles have been defined and expanded by Corey (1996, pp. 54–55) and can be best thought of as ways of working with clients. In essence, ethical practice involves engaging with clients in ways that:

- enhance well-being
- do not bring harm

- encourage independence
- are non-discriminatory, fair and equitable
- are honest and non-exploitative.

EXERCISE |

This is an exercise in fantasy aimed at assisting you to access, in a lived way, the pressing need for confidentiality in the therapeutic context. In order to develop an experiential understanding of this important issue you are asked to imagine a scene where you are exposed as having behaved in a way which you see as shameful. Before you begin you should find a comfortable, quiet space where you will not be disturbed. Sit comfortably and begin to notice and slow your breathing. Relax as much as you can, emptying your mind of the noise of the day. Where thoughts arise that interrupt this process of relaxation, simply note them and remind yourself that you can, and will, deal positively with them later. Once relaxed, begin your fantasy exercise.

Try now to think of a particular behaviour that might lead to feelings of shame, regret or disappointment in you. Picture the scene. Imagine what you were doing or had done and how you feel. Try hard to put yourself in this situation.

Make some brief notes below to record your thoughts. This material is sensitive – perhaps you should make notes that only you can understand or that are meaningful to you.

....

....

....

....

....

....

....

....

Having done this, imagine that it is six months later. The events have played on your mind, as things turned out far worse than you had anticipated. You feel distracted, exhausted and trapped by the past and decide to seek help through therapy.

Picture yourself in the third session of counselling with your therapist. Although initially helpful in dealing with the symptoms associated with your distress, you feel that you have reached an impasse. After thinking long and hard, you decide that the only way forward is to talk through the events which led to your distress. This means revealing the details of your past indiscretions and opening yourself up to the invalidation of someone whose opinion has come to matter. You are anxious and fearful about how your therapist will see you and what they may do with this disclosure.

You may stop now and de-role from the fantasy, reminding yourself how your life circumstances vary from those outlined above. Continue to relax and reflect on the feelings that arose in you while you were engaging in that activity.

In the space below note the thoughts and feelings that arose in you during the exercise, and in particular what you would have needed from your therapist to feel safe enough to take the risk of disclosure.

....

....

....

....

....

....

....

EXERCISE |

List below six positive therapist characteristics that would be necessary for you to have the confidence to disclose highly personal material:

1. ....

2. ....

3. ....

4. ....

5. ....

6. ....

In the above exercise you were encouraged to anticipate how it might feel to care deeply about the information someone may hold about you and the risks associated with disclosure or giving up control over information core to who you are. Such examples can help to sensitise us to the critical role we, as therapists, may have as the keepers of confidence of our client.

The following case study raises a range of challenges for the therapist. Read and reflect on the material before considering your answers to the questions in the exercise that follows.

Case study: Barbara

BACKGROUND

You work as a trainee counsellor in a large GP practice in London. You receive supervision for your work from a counselling psychologist whom you see weekly. The GP practice also employs a health visitor, and you have links with a broad range of health and welfare professionals in the community.

REFERRAL AND CLIENT DETAILS

Barbara is a 31-year-old Italian woman referred to you by her GP for counselling. The referrer hopes you may be able to complement his treatment of this depressed young woman through the provision of 'assertion training and interventions aimed at raising her self-esteem'. In addition to the prescribed anti-depressant medication, Barbara is also being treated for persistent stomach ulcers. The GP sees many of her problems stemming from her 'inability to stand up for herself'.

Barbara is the only surviving child of elderly Italian parents who moved from a northern Italian village to London some thirty years ago in the hope that their children could have a 'better future'. Sadly, one year after their arrival in England, Barbara's older brother was killed in a traffic accident while playing with neighbouring children.

After completing high school, Barbara attended a community college where she trained as a secretary. She found work easily and soon settled in at an accountancy firm within walking distance from her family home. Barbara continued to live at home until she married a junior associate whom she met at work. After they were married Barbara and her partner set up house two doors from her parents. Barbara describes this as the beginning of what was to be persistent marital conflict between her and her English husband.

Barbara's husband was never happy with the level of involvement she maintained with her parents. She reported that in order to 'break them up', he would demand that they never include her parents in their activities and he forbade her to telephone them. The breaking point came in their relationship when he applied for, and accepted, another job in the north of England. Barbara's husband expects her to leave London with him when the time comes for him to commence work. Barbara was devastated that he had made such a decision without consulting her. She sees no acceptable resolution to the dilemma that confronts her and feels like a failure, both as a daughter and a wife.

In an informal conversation with the GP, when he was enquiring about the progress of Barbara, he inadvertently disclosed to you that her mother was terminally ill. Barbara's mother had told neither her husband nor daughter of her poor prognosis and you immediately began to think that if Barbara had this information she would almost certainly choose to stay in London with her parents. That evening you found yourself agonising over what you might do with this information.

EXERCISE

Put yourself in the role of the therapist and think about your reactions to this case in terms of Corey's (1996) ethical principles. What would you do and why? How could your actions be understood or justified in terms of considerations of ethical decision-making?

1. I would..........(professional/ethical position)

....

....

....

....

....

2. I would like to.......(personal moral/value position)

....

....

....

....

....

....

3. Is there a conflict between your personal/moral stance and the requirements of ethical practice?

....

....

....

....

....

Personal morals and values aside, is there any conflict between the actions that might be suggested through the interpretation and application of Corey's (1996) guides for ethical practice? How might you act to:

Enhance Barbara's well-being

....

....

Not bring harm to Barbara

....

....

Encourage independence

....

....

Treat Barbara in a non-discriminatory, fair and equitable way

....

....

Demonstrate you are honest and non-exploitative

....

....

There are many excellent sources of discussion and debate relating to the topic of ethics (Bond, 2000). Rather than furnish you with a set of 'ethical rules' to equip you for therapeutic practice, this chapter aimed to provide you with the opportunity to experiment and apply a range of ethical principles to the case study. Thus it was ethical principles that were to be experimented with, rather than ethical rules. Rules imply a predictability of circumstances and such predictability typically eludes the therapist when working with real clients in the real world. The anticipation of the precise circumstance leading to an ethical dilemma is likely to remain an elusive, if not naive, goal. A knowledge and awareness of self, coupled with an understanding of the principles underlying ethical practice, will provide optimal security in the otherwise unpredictable and dynamic 'real world' of practice.

SUGGESTED FURTHER READING

Francis, R.D. (1999) *Ethics for Psychologists*. Leicester: BPS Books.
Tjeltveit, A.C. (1999) *Ethics and Values in Psychotherapy*. London: Routledge.

6

Personal strengths

What can I personally bring to the practice of therapy?

Undoubtedly one of the most commonly asked questions of trainee therapists is: 'What personal qualities do you have that will make you a good therapist?' Apart from cliché answers such as *I want to help people* and *I have always been a good listener*, there is a need to look at what personal strengths and weaknesses impact upon our work with clients. It has long been recognised that one's personal attributes affect not only one's work with clients but also one's own personal and professional development (Rogers, 1961). Indeed in recent years even therapeutic models, which in the past have placed little importance on the client–patient relationship, are now emphasising the value of personal attributes (McLeod, 1998). It has been suggested that the most important element in counselling is the 'personhood' of the counsellor (Gibson and Mitchell, 1999) and that the most powerful impact on the client may be that of observing what the counsellor is or does. The counsellor must be willing to invite the client to interact with a person (the counsellor) who is also struggling, evolving, risking, evaluating self, problem-solving and experiencing all the normal human emotions from grief to ecstasy.

Counselling is collaborative; it is something that two or more people create together. As such, trust and respect are integral parts of the working alliance. It is important for clients to perceive counsellors as people who are competent (but not perfect), mature, stable, continually learning and growing. These are the personal qualities that promote effective counselling. It is important too for clients to understand that counsellors are fallible and can experience ambivalence, failure, frustration and confusion. Unless counsellors work vigorously and systematically on self-evaluation and the resolution of their own problems, much of the therapeutic value of their contact with clients will be lost. Above all else, there is an abundance of research which suggests that therapist effectiveness has as much to do with the client's trust and belief in the therapist, as it does with the therapist's adherence to a particular theory of psychotherapy (McLeod, 1998).

There is no single and definitive list of personality strengths, rather there are paticular characteristics or attributes that each of us values about ourselves. The exercise below is intended to help you sharpen your focus on your own personal strengths.

Defining personal strengths

What does the term *personal strength* mean to you?

....

....

....

....

....

In a sentence, describe core personal strengths that a therapist should possess:

....

....

....

....

....

How in your opinion would the above description affect therapeutic work positively?

....

....

....

....

....

Can you see any way where the above definition might affect therapeutic negatively? If so how?

....

....

....

....

....

Name five people whom you admire for their personal strengths.

1...

2...

3...

4...

5...

What do the people you have named above have in common?

....

....

....

....

....

How do they differ?

....

....

....

....

....

Imagine that you are each of the people described in your list above; describe your personal strengths:

1.

....

....

....

2.

....

....

....

3.

....

....

....

4.

....

....

....

5.

....

....

....

Now, having read what you have written so far, make another attempt to write down what you feel are core personal strengths a therapist should possess:

....

....

....

....

....

....

....

....

PERSONAL THERAPY: EFFECTIVE COUNSELLORS, EFFECTIVE CLIENTS

Human beings are not static, we all have our peaks as well as our valleys and we all need someone to help us out at times. Gibson and Mitchell (1999) have suggested that learning to be effective clients enhances our effectiveness as counsellors. Much importance has been placed on the fact that counsellors cannot help clients when they themselves are anxious, depressed, or plagued by psychological or emotional distress.

Effective counselling cannot be separated from effective living. As such, effectiveness training should be a primary goal of every helper because effective living is the most valuable and powerful technique any counsellor can offer in a helping relationship. It is for this reason that personal therapy is a core requirement for the majority of psychological counselling and psychotherapy courses in Britain today. The belief underpinning the importance of this requirement revolves around three core principles. First, the notion that personal growth for the therapist is important; second, the idea that it is important for the therapist to gain empathic understanding of the client's position; and third, extending the trainee's experience of different types of therapy (Legg, 1998). However, although this is a core requirement, many trainees believe they do not need personal therapy and that this just adds to the pressure of training and course work assignments. Most trainers feel it is important for the counsellor to have the experience of being a client at some time, because at the very least such self-exploration can increase their level of self-awareness. Counsellors may find it useful or necessary to undergo personal therapy to overcome areas of difficulty which may compromise their counselling effectiveness. It is important therefore for trainees to understand why they should undergo personal therapy and what they can gain from the experience.

If you are undergoing personal therapy now or have done so in the past, go to Section 1; if you have not started personal therapy, go to Section 2. You should view the following questions as a prompt for your reflections. Record them in a personal log or journal, as they are likely to be of great interest to you in the years to come.

EXERCISE |

Section 1

1. Prior to going into therapy my expectations of the process were:

....

....

....

....

2. Prior to going into therapy I was anxious/worried about:

....

....

....

....

....

3. Prior to going into therapy my goals were:

....

....

....

....

....

4. What I value most about my relationship with my therapist is:

....

....

....

....

....

5. What I value most about my therapist is:

....

....

....

....

....

Section 2

1. My expectations of the therapy process are:

....

....

....

....

....

2. My apprehensions about going into therapy are:

....

....

....

....

....

3. My reason for going into therapy is:

....

....

....

....

....

4. My goals in therapy are likely to be:

....

....

....

....

....

5. What I am looking for in my relationship with my therapist is:

....

....

....

....

....

6. The personal quality I value most about a therapist is:

....

....

....

....

....

It has been suggested that our most powerful source of influencing clients in a positive direction is our living example of who we are and how we continually struggle to live up to our potential (Corey, 1996). It is also important to remain open to self-evaluation in order to expand one's awareness of one's self and to build the foundation for developing one's abilities as a professional. Therapy, because it is an intimate form of learning, demands a practitioner who is willing to shed stereotyped roles and be a real person in a relationship. If counsellors hide behind the safety of their professional role, their clients may actively work to keep themselves hidden from the counsellor.

In the exercise below, read the client's comment and respond to her by taking on the role of someone who you perceive to be an ineffectual counsellor (i.e. someone who does not possess personality traits that facilitate the therapeutic process).

EXERCISE |

Client: I feel that coming here was a mistake, I mean talking to a complete stranger about my problems... I know that you are a professional but you couldn't possibly know what it is like going through what I am feeling right now.

Ineffective therapist response:

....

....

....

....

....

Now respond to the same comment again, but this time take the role of a therapist who possesses all those personality traits you feel are conducive to a positive therapeutic relationship.

Effective therapist response:

....

....

....

....

....

What process did you have to go through to give each response? Describe the personality characteristics of each of the roles you took to respond to the client's comment:

....

....

....

....

....

How did you feel when constructing each of the responses?

....

....

....

....

....

In what way do the responses differ?

....

....

....

....

....

What effect do you imagine each of these responses would have had on the client?

....

....

....

....

....

Having completed this part of the exercise, what do you now feel are the most important personality traits a therapist should possess, and why?

....

....

....

....

....

Think of your own experiences as a trainee therapist so far: How do you see yourself and how would you like to see yourself in the future? In the boxes below make a list of your personal characteristics of your self now and your ideal self.

My real self   My ideal self

In view of the previous exercise, where have the ideal qualities been derived from?

....

....

....

Why are they ideal?

....

....

....

Could one still be a good therapist/person without these?

....

....

....

In asking how counsellors can be more 'therapeutic' and model growth and awareness for their clients, theorists have isolated a cluster of personal qualities and characteristics (Corey, 1996). The points raised are not intended to form a dogmatic protocol of the 'right' ways to be a therapist but are intended to encourage speculation as to what kind of person can make a significant difference in the lives of others.

Below is a list of fifteen characteristics believed to be important elements in the personality of a counsellor. Below each, write down whether you agree that this is an important characteristic in the personality of the therapist and give an example of how such traits might manifest themselves during counselling.

1. It is important that effective counsellors have a clear identity, but that they are willing to re-examine their values and goals.

....

....

....

2. Counsellors should have a clear sense of their priorities.

....

....

....

3. Effective counsellors respect and appreciate themselves and are able to recognise and accept their own power.

....

....

....

4. Counsellors should not feel the need to diminish others in order to experience a relative sense of power.

....

....

....

5. Effective counsellors may be open to change, constantly expanding their awareness of self and others.

....

....

....

6. Counsellors should be willing and able to tolerate ambiguity, as growth often depends on leaving the familiar and entering unknown territory.

....

....

....

7. Counsellors should be able to experience and know the world of the client and to be able to be sincere, authentic and honest.

....

....

....

8. Counsellors should not hide behind masks, defences, sterile roles and facades.

....

....

....

9. Counsellors must acknowledge that they make mistakes and be willing to admit them, and not to dismiss errors lightly or choose to ignore them.

....

....

....

10. Counsellors should be able to 'live in the present' and be able to experience the 'now' and appreciate the influence of culture.

....

....

....

11. Counsellors must develop their own unique style grounded in theory.

....

....

....

12. Counsellors should be able to put life events into perspective and should not have forgotten how to laugh, especially at their own foibles and contradictions.

....

....

....

13. Counsellors should be able to revitalise and re-create significant relationships. They should have the ability to reinvent themselves.

....

....

....

14. Counsellors should become deeply involved in their work and derive meaning from it. They can accept the rewards flowing from their work and they can honestly admit the ego needs that are gratified by it.

....

....

....

15. Counsellors should have a sincere interest in the welfare of others. This concern is based on respect, care, trust, and a real valuing of others. It implies that they are willing to challenge people who are significant in their lives to also remain open to growth.

....

....

....

In view of these fifteen statements, what do you think would be the most difficult aspect of living while adhering to the concepts described above?

....

....

....

....

....

THE ROLE OF VALUES IN COUNSELLING

A core issue is the degree to which a counsellor's values should enter into a therapeutic relationship. As counsellors, we are often taught not to let our values show, lest they bias the direction clients are likely to take. Yet we are simply not value-neutral, nor are we value-free; our therapeutic interventions rest on core values. Although our values do influence the way we practise, it is possible to maintain a sense of objectivity.

Answer the six questions below on the way that, in your view, a good counsellor approaches values.

EXERCISE

1. Should counsellors hold back their value judgements about their clients' choices? Is it possible for therapists to make value judgements only about events that affect their own personal life and pass no judgements on to clients?

....

....

....

....

....

2. How is it possible for a counsellor to disagree with a client's values and still accept him or her as a person?

....

....

....

....

....

3. How can practitioners retain their own sense of values and remain true to themselves, yet at the same time allow their clients the freedom to express values and behaviours that differ from and may even contradict the counsellors'?

....

....

....

....

....

4. What is the essential difference between counsellors who honestly expose their core values, when appropriate, and those who in subtle ways 'guide' their clients to accept the values they deem to be good for them?

....

....

....

....

....

5. What is the best course of action to take when the counsellor becomes aware of sharp value conflicts with certain clients?

....

....

....

....

....

6. Is it ever justifiable for counsellors to impose their values on clients? For instance, if a situation arises where the counsellor is convinced that the client's existing values result in self-destructive behaviour?

....

....

....

....

....

Looking at your answers above, how, if at all, can you separate a discussion of values from the therapeutic process?

....

....

....

....

....

The question of the influence of the counsellor's values on the client has ethical implications when we consider that goals and therapeutic methods are expressions of the counsellor's philosophy of life. Even though therapists should not directly teach the client or impose specific values, they do implement a philosophy of counselling, which is, in effect, a philosophy of life. Counsellors communicate their values by the therapeutic goals to which they subscribe and by the procedures they employ to reach these goals.

Counsellors' views of what they want their clients to be like, or their views of a healthy and optimally functioning person, do reveal their values. Because ethically sensitive therapists respect their clients' self-determination, they help them decide whether they are truly living by their values or merely incorporating parental and societal values without evaluating them. Professionals need to be alert to the possibility of manipulating a client to accept values wholesale, for to do so would mean that they were simply becoming another parent substitute.

Some counsellors contend that it is neither possible nor desirable for counsellors to be scrupulously neutral with respect to values in the counselling relationship (Corey, 1996). It has been suggested that counsellors should be willing to express their values openly when they are relevant to the questions that come up in their sessions. There can be a tendency to assume one of two extremes. At one extreme are counsellors who hold definite and absolute beliefs and see it as their job to exert influence on clients to adopt their values. These counsellors tend to direct their clients towards the attitudes and values they judge to be 'right'. At the other extreme are counsellors who maintain they should keep their values out of their work and that the ideal is to strive for value-free counselling. Because these counsellors are so intent on remaining objective and often are overly anxious not to influence their clients, they run the risk of immobilising themselves and appearing hollow and inauthentic.

Corey (1996) takes the position that clients often want and need to know where their therapist stands in order to critically examine their own thinking. Thus, it is argued, clients deserve an honest involvement on the part of their counsellor. Counselling is a process whereby clients are challenged to honestly appraise their values and then decide for themselves in what ways they will modify these values and their behaviour.

AVOIDING PERFECTIONISM

Both undergraduate students in human services and graduate students in counselling are prone to putting themselves under tremendous pressure. They tell themselves things such as 'I have to be the perfect counsellor, and if I'm not, I could do severe damage'; 'I should know everything there is to know about my profession, and if I show that there is something I don't know, others will see me as incompetent'; and 'I should always radiate confidence; there is no room for self-doubt'.

Perhaps one of the most common self-defeating beliefs with which we burden ourselves is that we must be perfect. Although we may well know intellectually that human beings are not perfect, emotionally we often feel there is little room for error. Counsellors who burden their minds with the constant thought that they must be perfect are in no way exhibiting a healthy personal attribute. Counsellors do not have to know everything and there is no disgrace in revealing their lack of knowledge. Rather than trying to impress others and bluffing their way through difficult situations, they can always acknowledge their deficits and set out to find the necessary information or answers (if indeed there is an answer).

To be sure, we will make mistakes, whether we are a beginning or a seasoned therapist. If we are tied up with presenting an image of perfection, there will be less energy left to be authentically with our clients.

EXERCISE ▌

Describe an event that you felt was a mistake you made with a client recently and give an account of why you think this event occurred.

....

....

....

....

....

On reflection, what have you learned from this event?

....

....

....

....

....

What is more important than our mistakes are the lessons we learn from those mistakes. It is important when training that therapists share their mistakes or perceived errors. If they are willing to make mistakes in supervised learning situations and to reveal their self-doubts, they will find a direction that leads to growth.

Many therapists fear facing their limitations as a practitioner. Counsellors fear losing the client's respect if they say 'I really feel that I can't help you on this point'. Clients' responses overwhelmingly confirm the value of honesty as opposed to an attempt to fake competence. Rather than lose their client's respect, counsellors who are authentic are more likely to earn their client's admiration for acknowledging their limitations.

From our own practice the following example comes to mind. A counsellor-in-training had intake duty in a college counselling centre. Her first client wanted to discuss the possibilities of an abortion for his girlfriend. Many questions raced through her mind: 'Should I admit to him my lack of knowledge about this issue or should I try to bluff my way through to avoid looking like a neophyte? Should I know how to help him? Will he give a negative impression of the counselling centre if I tell him that I don't have the skills to deal with this case? What about the girl in this situation? Is it really enough to work with only him?' Fortunately the counsellor-in-training let the client know that the matter was beyond her competence and she sensitively and efficiently referred him to an experienced colleague. The point of this illustration is that counsellors sometimes burden themselves with the expectation that they should be all-knowing and skilful, even without experience.

BOUNDARIES

The maintenance of healthy boundaries is critical if the problems of clients are not to be carried by the counsellors outside the session. Being an effective counsellor does not involve unbounded giving and altruism but the ability to say no, allowing the counsellor to keep a balance in his or her life. For a counsellor to show all the personal attributes we have covered here may seem monumental and unrealistic, but these points were not intended to be considered from an all-or-nothing perspective; rather, regard them on a continuum, and your capacity to exercise your competencies will vary across time and circumstance.

CONCLUSION

Although their personal characteristics are important, counsellors can be trained to improve in their ways of 'being with clients'. Indeed this capacity is inextricably linked to the characteristics reviewed in this chapter. Having good communication skills is not the same as being a good counsellor. An over-emphasis on communication skills can turn counselling into a lot of talk and very little action: technique can replace substance. Communication skills are essential of course, but they must always serve the outcomes of the helping process.

Nelson-Jones (1982) argues that, in an ideal world, counsellors would be models of the desired outcomes of their theoretical positions. However, Legg (1998) points out that the psychological limitations which affect clients may also apply to counsellors. When counsellors make decisions they can ignore relevant sources of information, under- or over-estimate the significance of events and often fail to carry out a complete analysis of the utilities of different choices. Counsellors are only human, and the best outcome of training will be the enhancement of personal strengths, the building of competency and the courage to embrace one's personal limits.

SUGGESTED FURTHER READING

Buhler, C. and Massarik, F.(eds) (1968) *The Course of a Human Life: A Study of Goals in the Humanistic Perspective*. New York: Springer.
Carlock, J.K. (1998) *Enhancing Self-Esteem* (3rd edn). London: Routledge.

7

Change and resistance to change

How do we know we are changing?

Therapy is about change. Change may be manifest in terms of an observable reorganisation of circumstances or relationships, or in the perspectives we take on these circumstances or relationships. The following exercises are designed to allow you the opportunity to experience the psychological and emotional processes that often accompany change. We also hope that they will provide a starting point from which to take your first steps towards some important revisions of your own personal circumstances or perspectives. Many of the exercises are rooted in George Kelly's (1955/1991) *Psychology of Personal Constructs*, and the interested reader is referred to the original source for further clarification of the theoretical constructs central to these change exercises. This chapter will deal in particular with concepts such as creativity, loosening your hold on cherished ideas or beliefs and turning insight into action.

CREATIVITY

Creativity is not just about finding novel and unconventional ways to view events; it is also about doing something with these insights. It is about the connection between thought, sense, feeling and action. The combination of insight and action requires a constant shift in perspective, a 'loosening' and 'tightening' of view. When one thinks about creativity, one is often drawn to the vision of the artist as one who generates an imaginative or ingenious 'slant' on events. Despite their diverse mediums, the painter, novelist, poet and sculptor all envision life in a particular fashion. Successful artists however have one thing in common: the skilful communication of their insight. Communication of insight requires operationalisation; that is, the putting of pen to paper, or brush and paint to canvas. The notion of loosening and tightening may be helpful in understanding processes of change. It is analogous to the generation of ideas and the implementation of strategies. What is critical here is a shift from insight to action. When one solves a problem, intellectual or emotional understanding alone is rarely enough. The implications of this insight must be acted upon. This putting theory into practice is what we will refer to here as 'tightening'. In this context, loose construing is the extravagant generation of ideas or perspectives, not limited by the realities of a lived set of personal circumstances.

The representation of loose construing in Figure 7.1 is illustrative of the process of circumspection, where one explores infinite possibilities undistracted by the pressure of outcomes or the need for absolute certainty. In the stylised figure the arrow can be seen exploring the contours of the circumstances that contain it.

Figure 7.1 A representation of loose construing[1] – meandering ideas

EXERCISE

Think of a time in your life when you were stuck, not because you could not think of a way forward, but rather you could not decide between a range of competing possibilities or options.

Make some notes to remind yourself of the circumstances.

....

....

....

....

....

What were the feelings associated with this set of circumstances?

....

....

....

1 The term *construing* is used to imply meaning-making practices such as thinking, feeling and sensing.

....

....

We will return to reflect on these feelings when we discuss common emotional experiences accompanying change.

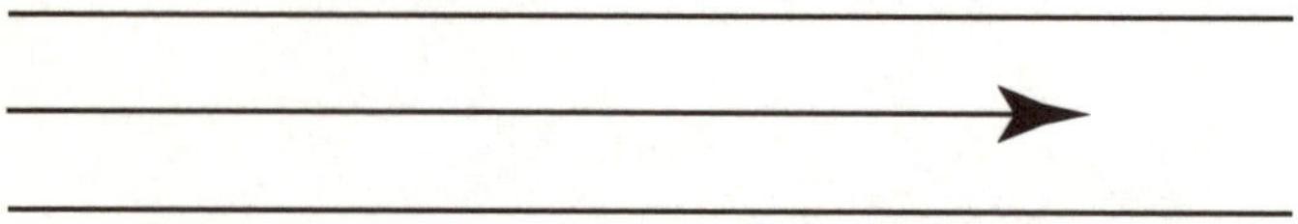

Figure 7.2 A representation of tight construing – clarity and rapid progress in the absence of obstacles

The representation in Figure 7.2 is illustrative of tight construing, or thinking clearly and unambiguously. The figure seeks to reflect the rapid progress that is made when one is able to anticipate a route with no obstacles or impediments. This style of thinking is characterised by a strong belief that you know what to do next. Seeing things in this way requires certainty and absolute confidence in your perspective.

EXERCISE |

Can you recall a time in your life when you thought you were sure how things would turn out, only to encounter an obstacle or unexpected opportunity? As in the preceding exercise, make some notes to remind you of the circumstances of that time.

....

....

....

....

....

What were the feelings associated with this set of circumstances?

....

....

....

Seeing things too tightly or too loosely is likely to get us into trouble from time to time. It is optimal to utilise some combination or alternation from loose to tight or tight to loose if we seek to maintain the sort of active flexibility that is required to live effectively in the world. Figure 7.3 gives a snapshot of this endless shifting between tight and loose construing.

Thus when we encounter problems in our lives it is sometimes because we are stuck in one of these phases of thinking. Imagine the person who can see endless possibilities, challenges and opportunities in every set of circumstances. This is clearly a strength, but a qualified strength. If every option is to be explored in the knowledge that there are likely to be many more options not yet dreamed of, then the individual is unlikely to act for fear that a still better solution may be conceived. Here creativity can be seen as a barrier to action and a handicap to change.

Where the individual opts for a tried and true course of action, as in the case of tight construing, there is a high likelihood of speedy success (if all goes to plan). In the event of an unanticipated complication, the 'tight construer' is stuck without an alternative. This often manifests as the individual trying harder at a strategy already demonstrated to be a failure. We are probably familiar with the frustrated native speaker who raises their voice in an attempt to communicate directions or instructions to the non-native speaker. The problem here is not audibility, the tourist has no problem hearing; it is comprehension, the tourist simply does not understand the language. In such circumstances no matter how loud or how frequently the frustrated native speaker repeats themselves their efforts will be in vain. Strategies such as these, where we persist with the same behaviour despite its failure to secure the desired outcome, were described by Kelly (1955/1991) as 'hostility' or the failure to give up what does not work. The overly loose construer in such a circumstance might wrestle endlessly with which route is the best and therefore fail to offer any suggestion with the clarity and confidence the anxious traveller requires before setting out on their journey into the unknown.

We have already mentioned 'hostility', or the holding on to beliefs longer than we should, and 'anxiety' as the experience of not being able to understand what has just happened or to predict what will happen next. In reviewing the events

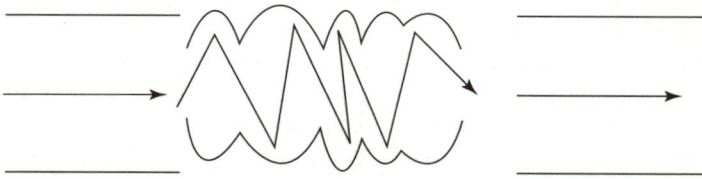

Figure 7.3 Movement from tight to loose *ad infinitum*

you recalled in relation to the 'tight' and 'loose' construing exercise, did you experience any other emotions which Kelly (1955/1991) saw as commonly accompanying periods of change or transition? These emotional experiences are defined in the following exercise. Indicate which were experienced during the circumstances you previously described by placing a tick in the adjacent box.

EXERCISE |

Anxiety: the experience of not being able to understand what has just happened or to predict what will
happen next.

Hostility: the tendency to persist with the same
behaviour despite its failure to secure a desired outcome or a reluctance to give up what does not work.

Threat: the awareness that some deeply held belief
about the world, yourself or others has turned out not
to be true.

Guilt: catching a glimpse of yourself behaving in ways
that are not how you want others to see you or as you
want to see yourself.

Aggression: a hunger or drive to explore and chart new
territory involving the testing of limits or orthodox
boundaries.

UNDERSTANDING WHY THINGS MATTER

If we take the view that everything we do we do for a good reason, then a natural curiosity regarding why we sometimes do things that are not in our best interests is likely to arise. All of us can probably identify a fairly extensive list of achievable goals that are materially and practically within our reach but that continue to elude us. For some it is continuing to smoke after making a declaration to stop. For others it might be a resolve to go regularly to the gym or complete assignments well in advance of the deadline. So why do we fail to do what we believe to be admirable or desirable? The answer to this perplexing question rests in the implications attached to our desired goal. Events like smoking, exercise and punctuality do not occur in isolation; rather they are embedded in a network of implications, some positive and some negative. These implications may appear invisible to us and routinely outside of our awareness. Dennis Hinkle (1965) developed a techinque which he called 'laddering' in order to shed some light on this very human tendency.

Laddering is a technique which is based on the assumption that some personal values, preferences or beliefs are more important than others. Laddering provides us with a way of exploring why individuals make the choices they do or why seemingly innocuous events or circumstances debilitate them. The laddering technique is simple to implement; however, this should not distract us from exercising caution in its application. You will quickly gain access to core personal values and hence be provided with the opportunity to make links between your own thinking, feeling and behaviour.

EXERCISE |

Steps to laddering

1. Identify the topic of interest. It might be smoking versus not smoking or going to the gym versus relaxing at home. For the purpose of the exercise it is important to crystallise both topic of interest and its opposite.

2. Ask yourself which of this pair you prefer. Would it be going to the gym or relaxing at home?

3. Having identified which you prefer, ask yourself: *What is the most important thing about this, and why do I prefer it?*

4. Record what you believe to be the best thing about your choice and then ask yourself what the opposite of this implication is.

5. Repeat steps 2 and 3, identifying which of the two options you prefer.

6. This process should be repeated until you can no longer come up with a new implication. Such a situation will often manifest itself with you saying to yourself something like, 'It just is. That is the most important thing.' Such core values and beliefs are sometimes without an adequate verbal label.

The example given in Figure 7.4 was the product of a dilemma experienced by a client who could not make up her mind about where to spend Christmas day. Step 1 is recorded at the base of the figure in terms of the dilemma whether to spend Christmas with family or Christmas with friends. The implications, which were seen by this young person as positive, have been circled. The question mark represents an implicative dilemma and the large tick indicates her final choice.

From the lowest level of the ladder it is clear that the client, on first thought, would prefer to spend Christmas with her friends; however, she cannot decide what she should do (second stage of the ladder). As you review the higher levels of the ladder it becomes clear that although she might prefer to spend Christmas with her friends she will worry about her family, and as a consequence feel guilty and 'bad'.

Our client in the above example is able to appreciate that it 'makes sense' that she is confused, and that she is not 'crazy' for not just spending Christmas with her friends – like everyone else she knows.

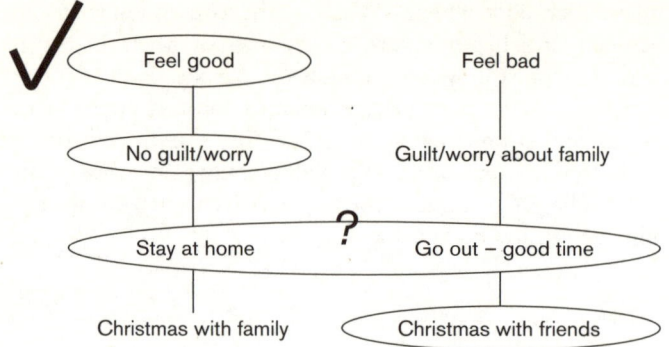

Figure 7.4 Steps to laddering: an example

EXERCISE ▐

It is time for you to put the strategy of laddering into action. For the purposes of this exercise identify a habit or behaviour of a significant other that annoys or frustrates you. Where possible, identify a behaviour you know is likely to escape the attention of most others and where you could be accused of 'over-reacting'. Once you have come up with this habit or behaviour place it at the bottom of the ladder next to Point 1. Ask yourself what is the opposite of this habit and place your response adjacent to Point 1a. Now refer to the instructions for laddering and complete the exercise.

5. _____ vs 5a. _____

4. _____ vs 4a _____

3. _____ vs 3a. _____

2. _____ vs 2a. _____

1. _____ vs 1a _____

Once you have completed the exercise you should have developed a clearer understanding of why you feel as strongly as you do about something that many may see as trivial. You concede that the event itself may be conceived as trivial, but the meaning attached to it has profound implications for you. Having insight into your own processes of meaning-making enables you to critically appraise your reaction to events and mediate your responses accordingly.

SUGGESTED FURTHER READING

Brammer, L.M. (1991) *How to Cope with Life Transitions: The Challenge of Personal Change*. New York: Hemisphere.

Carlock, J.K. (1998) *Enhancing Self-Esteem: Third Edition*. London: Routledge.

Harvey, J.H. (2000) *Give Sorrow Words: Perspectives on Loss and Trauma*. London: Brunner-Routledge.

Conclusion

What have we learned and what now: do we know we don't know?

Helping another human being is a process of enabling. It is a process through which both the counsellor and the client encounter opportunities to grow. This book has aimed to provide a vehicle within which to engage in self-exploration around topics fundamental to the practice of counselling and therapy.

Helpers are human beings with idiosyncratic needs and desires. These needs and desires become problematic only when they are expressed without awareness of how they might adversely affect our clients. When appropriately expressed, they enable us to be real in the helping relationship, while minimising the risks of influencing clients to make choices that may have more to do with our prejudices than their preferences.

THE COUNSELLOR'S DEVELOPMENT

The categorisation and identification of the skills and qualities associated with effectiveness in counselling have largely focused on competencies exhibited by people who are already practitioners. However, one does not become a counsellor by sitting an examination or taking a course alone; rather it is a process of recursive and ongoing personal and professional development. Many counsellors find meaning in the metaphor of the 'counsellor's journey' (Goldberg, 1988), an image which allows them to trace the roots of their counselling role back to its earliest origins, and to make sense of the different territories and obstacles encountered on the way to becoming a counsellor. The personal and professional pathways followed by counsellors are divisible into five distinct and overlapping stages:

1. Roles, relationship patterns and emotional needs established in childhood.

2. The decision to become a counsellor.

3. The experience of training.

4. Coping with the hazards of practice.

5. Expressing creativity in the counselling role.

This model draws on research mainly carried out in the USA (Henry, 1977), although there is some evidence of the relevance of the model for British counsellors (Norcross and Guy, 1989). The final stage of this model emphasises the endless scope for growth, development and lifelong learning inseparable from the role of therapist. The development of an identity as an independent counsellor is an area that has received little attention in this book. It is the very major and ongoing next step for all trainees and one that will remain always in the making.

Certain childhood experiences have been seen as creating the conditions for embarking on a career as a therapist. Brightman (1984) noted that 'the role of therapist itself may constitute a re-enactment of an earlier situation in which a particularly sensitive and empathetic child has been pressed into the service of understanding and caring for a parent figure'. The child, Brightman hypothesised, grows up with a need to care for others. As the sibling most involved in the family drama, he or she is not able to escape from the responsibility to care. The experience of being a social outsider introduces the additional motivation to learn about and understand relationships and interactions.

The pattern of childhood and adult experience is unique for every therapist and undoubtedly shapes one's approach to the practice of counselling as a career. Marston (1984) suggests that the motives for becoming a therapist may include contact, helping others, discovery, social status, power and influence, self-therapy and even voyeurism. Clearly, some motives are more problematic than others. For perhaps the majority of counsellors, the pathway into the occupation unfolds over time. It is common for people to enter professions such as nursing, social work and teaching and then find themselves more and more attracted to, and involved in, the counselling components of the job. Undergoing personal therapy or counselling as a client may also be the catalyst for the decision to enter counselling training, while the experience of meeting therapists or trainers who become influential role models may also be a factor. The decision to become a counsellor may be prompted or facilitated by any number of events or influences, and it is hoped that through the use of this book you have been assisted in identifying how you got to be where you are today.

Once a person has decided to become a counsellor and enters formal training, they inevitably face the dreaded question: 'Am I good enough?' Answering in the affirmative requires a confidence in one's own groundedness, theoretical and personal knowledge and competence. Crises of confidence are common in the early years of training, particularly when personal fears of adequacy are compounded by the complexity and uniqueness of clients. Counsellors in training and counsellors post-training will at times feel vulnerable and incompetent. Dealing with fear and a desire to do the best one can remain lifelong challenges. The absence of anxiety may not be wholly positive. Appropriate supervision, personal reflection and personal therapy can facilitate the resolution of periods of transitory anxiety and enhance our capacity to work creatively with clients.

In selecting candidates for counsellor training, a crucial question is whether the person is ready to give help to others or whether he or she is more needy of therapy him- or herself. In training, a principal task is to acknowledge vulnerability and accept the 'negative capability' of not knowing everything. For qualified practitioners, competence is contingent upon periodic renewal and discovery of personal meaning in their work. As McConnaughy (1987) noted, the actual techniques employed by counsellors are of lesser importance than the unique character and personality of the therapists themselves. Therapists select techniques and theories because of who they are as persons: the therapy strategies are manifestations of the therapist's personality. The therapist as a person is the instrument of primary influence in the therapy enterprise. A corollary of this principle is that the more a therapist accepts and values him- or herself, the more effect he or she will have in helping clients come to know and appreciate themselves.

Change and self-discovery that occur in a counsellor's life are crucial to how that counsellor operates. Counsellors learn and discover just as do their clients, and it is important that they are able to assimilate and accommodate the processes of change in order for them to achieve and maintain optimal effectiveness.

CONCLUSION

One of the basic issues in the counselling profession concerns the significance of the counsellor as a person in the therapeutic relationship. Since counsellors are asking people to take an honest look at themselves and to make choices concerning how they want to change, it is critical that counsellors themselves be open to the same kind of personal scrutiny.

Counsellors should repeatedly ask themselves questions such as 'What do I personally have to offer others who are struggling to find their way? Am I prepared to test my professional theories on myself?' Counsellors can acquire an extensive theoretical and practical knowledge and can make that knowledge available to their clients, but to every therapeutic session they bring themselves as individuals. They bring their human qualities and the life experiences that have moulded them. It is possible that professionals are well versed in psychological theory and can learn diagnostic and interviewing skills and still be ineffective as helpers. If counsellors are to promote growth and change in their clients, they must be willing to promote growth in their own lives by exploring their own choices and decisions, and by striving to become aware of the ways in which they may maximise their own potential for growth. The willingness to attempt to live in accordance with what they teach and thus to be positive models for their clients is what makes counsellors 'therapeutic persons'.

One cannot know at the outset what one does not know, and as such the following inventory is offered as an opportunity to evaluate the change you have undergone through the completion of this manual. The items, which constitute the inventory, are adapted from Dryden *et al.* (1995, pp.98-99), and set out a range of dimensions which those authors see as critical to personal and professional development. Against each question you are asked to indicate whether you think your insight or understanding has grown through the completion of this manual, or whether your understanding of the dimension in question remains unchanged.

	Dimension of personal and professional development	Unchanged	Changed
1	Aware of values and beliefs that were uncritically adopted from others which influence self-concept and behaviour		
2	Aware of the social influences on available meanings		
3	Understand how social and personality dynamics have influenced my development		
4	Understand the 'conditions of worth' which operated in my early development and influence me today		
5	Understand when I am experiencing change and resistance to change		
6	Possess a strong sense of identity		
7	Aware of enduring patterns in my own behaviours and interpersonal relationships		
8	Aware of the basis of my needs and fears that have given rise to personal biases		
9	Aware of how my own sexuality is expressed through personal and professional relationships		
10	Aware of my own theory of human behaviour		
11	Aware of any personal blocks I may possess that will inhibit equality in the therapeutic relationship		
12	Aware of ways in which my personal preferences and prejudices may enter the counselling setting		
13	Aware of blocks to personal development		
14	Aware of the conditions which may place me at risk of over-involvement with clients		
15	Aware of the conditions which may place me at risk of under-involvement with clients		
16	Ability to develop personal learning goals		
17	A disposition to critically examine understanding of skills and attitudes		
18	Confidence to tolerate and learn from challenge to own value system		
19	Confidence to own one's behavioural choices		
20	Ability to accept and respond to the feedback of others		
21	Ability to appraise self openly and accurately		

Where you have indicated that any dimension remains unchanged following the completion of this manual, you should determine whether this is because that particular dimension was either a pre-existing personal strength, or an appropriate target for future development. Where change has occurred, you should praise your openness to experience and willingness to engage in the process of personal and professional development. Where change has not occurred and you believe your practice would be enhanced by further exploration of this particular dimension of personal development, celebrate your insight. It is critical to acknowledge that growth and development are lifelong processes. It would be worrying indeed if, at this point, you believed you had arrived at a place of absolute resolution and integration, where no further work or exploration was required. We genuinely wish you well in your continuing growth and development up to and throughout your practice as a therapist.

Finding a counsellor or personal therapist

National Register of Psychotherapists
United Kingdom Council for Psychotherapy
167–169 Great Portland Street
London W1N 5FB
Tel: 020 7436 3002
Fax: 020 7436 3013
www.psychotherapy.org.uk

Counselling and Psychotherapy Resource Directory
British Association for Counselling and Psychotherapy
1 Regent Place
Rugby
Warwickshire
CV21 2PJ
Tel: 0870 443 5252
Fax: 0870 443 5160
www.counselling.co.uk

The Directory of Chartered Psychologists
The British Psychological Society
St Andrews House
48 Princess Road East
Leicester LE1 7DR
Tel: 0116 254 9568
Fax: 0116 247 0787
www.bps.org.uk

References

Albino Gilbert, L. and Scher, M. (1999) *Gender and Sex in Counseling and Psychotherapy*. London: Allyn & Bacon.

Aveline, M.O. (1986) Personal themes from training groups for health care professionals. *British Journal of Medical Psychology*, 59, 325–335.

Beck, A. (1976) *Cognitive Therapy and Emotional Disorders*. New York: New American Library.

Beck, R.L. (1987) Genogram as a process. *The American Journal of Family Therapy*, 15, 343–352.

Becker, L.C. and Becker, C.B. (1992) *Encyclopedia of Ethics*. London: St James Press.

Bem, S.L. (1993) *The Lenses of Gender: Transforming the Debate on Sexual Inequality*. New Haven, CT: Yale University Press.

Blackburn, S. (1996) *Oxford Dictionary of Philosophy*. New York: Oxford University Press.

Bond, T. (2000) *Standards and Ethics for Counselling in Action*. London: Sage.

Brightman, B.K. (1984) Narcissistic issues in the training experience of the psychotherapist. *International Journal of Psychoanalytic Psychotherapy*, 10, 293–371.

Buckley, W. (1967) *Sociology and Modern Systems Theory*. Englewood Cliffs, NJ: Prentice Hall.

Burr, V. and Butt, T. (1996) *Invitation to Personal Construct Psychology*. London: Whurr.

Coleman, E. (1990) Toward a synthetic understanding of sexual orientation, in D.P. McWhirter, A.A. Sanders and J.M. Reinisch (eds) *Homosexuality/ Heterosexuality: Concepts of Sexual Orientation*. New York: Oxford University Press.

Corey, G. (1996) *Theory and Practice of Counselling and Psychotherapy*. Belmont, CA: Brooks/Cole.

Corsini, R. J. (ed.) (1981) *Handbook of Innovative Psychotherapies*. New York: Wiley.

Dryden, W., Horton, I. and Mearns, D. (1995) *Issues in Professional Counsellor Training*. London: Cassell.

Egan, G. (1986) *The Skilled Helper. A Systematic Approach to Effective Helping* (3rd edn). Belmont, CA: Brooks/Cole.

Gaines, A.D. (1982) Cultural definitions, behaviour and the person in American psychiatry, in A.J. Marsella and G. White (eds), *Cultural Concepts of Mental Health and Therapy*. Dordrecht: Reidel.

Gibson, R.L. and Mitchell, M.H. (1999) *Introduction to Counselling and Guidance*. London: Prentice Hall.

Goldberg, C. (1988) *On Being a Psychotherapist: The Journey of the Healer*. New York: Gardner Press.

Harway, M. (1979) Training Counsellors. *Counselling Psychologist*, 8, 8–10.

Henry, W.E. (1977) Personal and social identities of psychotherapists, in A.S. Gurman and A.M. Razin (eds), *Effective Psychotherapy: A Handbook of Research*. Oxford: Pergamon Press.

Hinkle. D.N. (1965) *The Change of Personal Constructs from the Viewpoint of a Theory of Construct Implications*. Unpublished Ph.D. dissertation, The Ohio State University, Ohio, USA.

Kareem, J. and Littlewood, R. (eds) (1992) *Intercultural Therapy – Themes, Interpretations and Practice*. Oxford: Blackwell Scientific.

Kelly, G.A. (1955/1991) *The Psychology of Personal Constructs*, vols 1 and 2. London: Routledge.

Kinsey, A.C., Pomeroy, W.B., Martin, C.E. and Gebhard, P.H. (1953) *Sexual Behavior in the Human Female*. Philadelphia, PA: W.B.Saunders.

Kleinman, A. (1988) *The Illness Narratives: Suffering, Healing and the Human Condition*. New York: Basic Books.

Kovacs, A.L. (1976) The emotional hazards of teaching psychotherapy. *Psychotherapy*, 13, 321–334.

Legg, C. (1998) *Psychology and the Reflective Counsellor*. Leicester: BPS Books.

Leong, F.T.L. and Kim, H.H.W. (1991) Going beyond cultural sensitivity on the road to multiculturalism: using the intercultural sensitiser as a counselling training tool. *Journal of Counselling and Development*, 70, 112–118.

Luborsky, L., Singer, B. and Luborsky, L. (1975) Comparative studies of psychotherapies: is it true that 'everyone has one and all must have prizes'? *Archives of General Psychiatry*, 32, 995–1008.

McGoldrick, M. and Gerson, R. (eds) (1985) *Genograms in Family Assessment*. New York: Norton.

McConnaughy, E.A. (1987) The person of the therapist in therapeutic practice. *Psychotherapy*, 24, 303–314.

McLeod, C. (1998) *An Introduction to Counselling Psychology*. Milton Keynes: Open University Press.

Mair, M. (1989) *Between Psychology and Psychotherapy: A Poetics of Experience*. London: Routledge.

Marmor, J. (1953) The feeling of superiority: an occupational hazard in the practice of psychotherapy. *American Journal of Psychiatry*, 110, 370–376.

Marston, A.R. (1984) What makes therapists run? A model for the analysis of motivational styles. *Psychotherapy*, 21, 456–459.

Nelson-Jones, R. (1982) *The Theory and Practice of Counselling Psychology*. New York: Holt, Rinehart & Winston.

Norcross, J.C. and Guy, J.D. (1989) Ten therapists: the process of becoming and being, in W. Dryden and L. Spurling (eds), *On Becoming a Psychotherapist*. London: Tavistock/Routledge.

Papadopoulos, L. (1995) The impact of illness on the family and family's impact on illness. *Counselling Psychology Quarterly*, 8, 27–30.

Papadopoulos, L. and Bor, R. (1995) Counselling psychology in primary health care: a review. *Counselling Psychology Quarterly*, 8, 1–30.

Richardson, T. and Helms, J.E. (1994) The relationship of the racial identity attitudes of black men to perceptions of 'parallel' counselling dyads. *Journal of Counselling and Development*, 73, 172–177.

Ridley, C.R. (1995) *Overcoming Unintentional Racism in Counselling and Psychotherapy*. Thousand Oaks, CA: Sage.

Rogers, C.R. (1961) *On Becoming a Person*. Boston, MA: Houghton Mifflin.

Rolland, J. (1984) Toward a psychosocial typology of chronic and life-threatening illness. *Family Systems Medicine*,11, 201–208.

Ross, M.W. and Paul, J.P. (1992) Beyond gender: the basis of sexual attraction in bisexual men and women. *Psychological Reports*, 71, 1283–1290.

Sharaf, M.R. and Levinson, D.J. (1964) The quest for omnipotence in professional training. *Psychiatry*, 27, 135–149.

Storms, M.D. (1981) A theory of erotic orientation development. *Psychological Review*, 88, 340–353.

Strupp, H. (1978) The therapist's theoretical orientation: an overrated variable. *Psychotherapy*, 15, 314–317.

Sue, D.W. and Sue, D. (1990) *Counselling the Culturally Different* (2nd edn). Chichester: Wiley.

Sue, D.W., Aredondo, P. and McDavis, R.J. (1992) Multicultural counselling competencies and standards: a call to the profession. *Journal of Counselling and Development*, 70, 477–486.

Tomson, P. (1985) Genograms in general practice. *Journal of the Royal Society of Medicine* (Supplement), 78, 34–39.

Welfel, E.R. and Kitchener, K.S. (1992) Introduction to the special section: Ethics education: an agenda for the 90's. *Professional Psychology Research and Practice*, 23, 179–181.

Woolfe, R. and Dryden, W. (eds) (1996) *Handbook of Counselling Psychology*. London: Sage.

Index

Note: page numbers in *italics* refer to figures, page numbers in **bold** refer to tables.

action 88–9
Afro-Caribbeans 31
aggression 92
ambiguity 79
anti-racism 46
anticipation 2
'anxiety' 91, 92
Aredondo, P. 39
assumptions 32, 33
attitudes
    of culturally skilled therapists 39
    of ethnic minorities to counselling 28

Beck, R.L. 25
beliefs, of culturally skilled therapists 39
biases, therapists' 32, 33, 39, 40
bisexuality 56, **56**
black people 31, 37, 38
boundaries 86–7
Brightman, B.K. 97
Buckley, W. 6

caring, as need 97
case studies
    ethical issues 64–6
    gender issues 54–5
    genograms 25–6
causality 3
change 88–95, 98–9, 100
    and creativity 88–92
    familial 24
    and 'loose' construing 88–9, 89, 91–2,
        91
    openness to 79
    resistance to 88–95
    and 'tight' construing 88–9, 90–2, 90,
        91

understanding why things matter 92–4
childhood experiences, and the decision to
    become a therapist 97
coincidence, of dates 22
Coleman, E. 57
collaboration 68
Collins, Clare 25–6
Collins, James 25–6
commitment 2
competence 39–40, 98
confidence, crises of 97
confidentiality 62–4
confirmation 2
constructive revision 3
Corey, G. 61, 66, 85
'counsellor's journey' 96
creativity 88–92
cultural difference 28, 32–3, 36–44, 46
cultural training model 44–6
culture 28–47
    and competency 39–40
    critiques of existing multicultural
        approaches 44–6
    incorporation into counselling practice
        40–1
    and interpretation of behaviour 31–3
    and racism 33–8, 40
    skilled therapists 39–40
    and therapeutic limitations 41–2
    therapists' assumptions about 30–1,
        38–9, 42–3
    welcolming diversity 41–4

dates, coincidences of 22
decision making, becoming a therapist 97
diagnosis, mental illness in ethnic
    minorities 28